To Dad

GW01237923

On yo

They say "everyone has
a book in them waiting
to be written"

BELFAST

But I think Atan beat
you to it.

Hope this brings you
more laughter than tears.

Love,

Tim

19/03/17

Belfast

TEARS AND LAUGHTER 1957-1977

Alan Croft

MILL CITY PRESS, MINNEAPOLIS

Mill City Press, Inc.
322 First Avenue N, 5th floor
Minneapolis, MN 55401
612.455.2293
www.millcitypublishing.com

ISBN-13: 978-1-63413-409-5
LCCN: 2015903600

Cover Design by Alan Pranke
Typeset by Mary K. Ross

Printed in the United States of America

This book is dedicated to my great friends Billy Caughey and Michael Donaldson, who both died within a year of each other while I was still writing, and also to all the characters I grew up with on the housing estate that made writing the book easy.

Also with thanks to my wife Nancy and sons Sam (the editor) and Bobby.

CONTENTS

PREFACE

Autobiographies seem to be reserved for the rich or famous but the everyday life of an average person can be just as interesting and important. After all we are all the same when we are dead. I think it would be a good idea for each and every person to give a detailed account of his or her life, from earliest memories to middle age when it's really not worth noting anymore. Just as you would fill in a time sheet for a week worked this would be a time sheet for a life lived. I expect most of the stories would be a great big bore but every now and then you'd get something good.

Young children love to hear stories of their parents' pasts, so why not document it for them or anyone else to read? Not all is known of a parent's background; very little of a grandparent's background; and what of the life of a great grandparent? Most of us know nothing at all of these mysterious relatives from the olden days: what they looked like, where they lived and worked. They tread the earth a mere three generations ago; it's not as if they witnessed the fall of Rome.

Middle age can be a tough time, particularly for women during menopause, but it can also be quite difficult for men. They can also suffer from this affliction although male menopause is not as obvious as the female version. There are no hot flashes, no getting away with murder because the change is happening: a change much like becoming a werewolf only with not as much hair. Most men will never admit there is anything going wrong and a lot slip into depression without realizing it and attempt to carry on with life when really they should be looking for help. Try getting a grumpy middle-aged man to admit he is close to becoming a mental case. It is passed off as a midlife crisis and some decide to fight it by getting tattoos or matching ear and nose rings to go along with the grey ponytails that dangle from the backs of their leathery bald heads like donkey's arses. Others blow vast sums of money getting their wrinkly old faces stretched or thatches for their chrome domes to make them look younger, only to see it all blown away when they take their first trips in their recently-purchased expensive sports cars. Beware of those baldy or greying old wankers farting around in high performance automobiles commandeering the middle lane doing about 60 MPH.

Personally, there was something not right inside me but I could not accept it was depression until my wife Nancy suggested politely that I should see a shrink. After all you had to be nuts to be depressed and I had a record of being no more than slightly inconsistent at times, so I took up the challenge – I'd show this witch doctor that I was perfectly fine. The therapist was a last resort – as opposed to an all inclusive resort on the Italian Riviera – and I was hoping he could guide me to a light at the end of a dark tunnel. There was no money available for me to join the *flash car brigade* to help me disguise my plight so off I went to the comfy couch. My problem was that I felt life seemed just mediocre: get on with it and get it over. Little interested me and I looked forward to absolutely nothing. I wasn't close to being suicidal but if it all ended that day then: so what? Not the greatest way to feel in my 50's.

What I did get out of this learned shrink was the satisfaction that he really wanted to listen – or at least he convinced me that he was listening. No one else seemed to so why not bore the arse off someone who was paid to do it? He would let me ramble on about my past, a lot of which was buried deep in my memory bank. I had never bothered anyone before with these tales of dark days gone by in the years I had spent growing up during the Troubles of Belfast, so it was a pleasing experience: one that I enjoyed and one that I actually looked forward to doing again. It was definitely progress on my part.

"Keep talking about Belfast," the doctor requested.

He was convinced that something from my past was affecting my present. There had been a few traumatic events that had occurred back then and although the chaos had been normal at that time it now seemed strangely unreal. These sessions with the doctor were the encouragement I needed to start writing and it was certainly better therapy than medication.

INTRODUCTION

The following account is a recollection of events from my childhood to the year when I ultimately left Belfast in an effort to change my way of life and leave behind the upside-down world that was Northern Ireland. They are as accurate as my fading memory can recall. It illustrates how the tranquil early years would end, thus forever altering not only my personality but also the personalities of countless others who lived through those times. Looking back I find it hard to believe that life went on as normally as possible considering the turmoil that ensued as the people of Ulster adapted to survive. Why was there so much hatred between two sets of people? How could people born so close to each other be so far apart? Although raised on the same island they are educated with completely different agendas that transform them into two separate races: the Protestants are brought up British and the Catholics as Irish. During my years away from Northern Ireland meeting Catholics from Ulster whilst living in both England and Canada I found that if the past is left behind then we are exactly the same. Almost.

PART ONE

CHAPTER 1

The Early Days

A red Morris 1100 swerved aggressively in the misty damp night as it rounded the corner close to where Sam and I walked unsteadily on our way home from the pub. Seconds later one short burst of automatic gunfire had us instinctively dive in unison over a hedge into the garden below. After crawling out we cautiously made our way to an army checkpoint at the top of the hill. Just beyond the barrier the car lay prone: rear window shattered; front end crumpled against a lamp pole. On the back seat two passengers sat slumped against each other.

The night was now silent as the soldiers approached the car with their rifles still pointed towards the motionless youths. One soldier instructed us to halt and we did so. It was difficult to distinguish between the paintwork of the car

1

and the blood that had ruptured forth from the gaping head wounds. There was no moaning or groaning, no movement at all. The end result was four youngsters shot: three died instantly and one was to die later in hospital. All were just 17 or 18.

It sounds like the opening lines of a novel – a thriller – but it was real life, it was a real tragedy and I was watching it take place. I was the same age as the young victims.

"They're taidy bread," said Sam as we shrugged our shoulders and passed on by. Just another Belfast statistic.

Their crime was joyriding. This was Belfast in the 1970's. Maybe the soldiers should have been accountable for their actions but they lived on a razor's edge. Life or death to them could be a split second decision and the joyriders knew the risks of running checkpoints – but that was part of the high. That scene of the dead youths will be engraved in my mind for eternity. This was just one of many moments growing up in strife-torn Belfast that sadly became a normal way of life. When I look back to that time it seems as if it never really happened, probably because I put the memories on a backburner and everything had been subconsciously erased from the day I left Belfast. I would avoid any discussions on the subject of the Troubles during my years in England and Canada. It now felt like the right time to remember again and to write about how my life had changed considerably from those turbulent early days until now: the mundane present.

It all began on May 14th, 1957. I was born the grandson of the famous Tucker Croft, a man who scored the winning goal for Ireland in a 2-1 victory over England in 1923 that made him one of football's immortals. I was the first of two children born to wonderful parents at Malone Place Hospital and I arrived not long after Humphrey Bogart had smoked his final cigarette. The old hospital was a beautiful building: clean and friendly with its main doors opening out onto the educated part of the Lower Lisburn Road. A walk through the back entrance however was a different kettle of fish as you strayed onto one of Belfast's toughest roads: Sandy Row. I think this is how my early teens were played out: stuck between some of the nicest possible people and some of the most unstable people to walk this earth. Two years later, also in May, my sister joined the family. In an effort not to cause confusion with my mother, my great aunt or my cousin, all of whom were called Kathleen, the new arrival was named: Kathleen. We would become great playmates as we grew and travelled with our parents, though we did squabble occasionally – and she usually won.

I am not sure just how far back I can remember. Sometimes a yarn from my mother or father would confuse me; was this something I actually recalled or was this just a story from my parents? Traumatic experiences undoubtedly stay with us; my earliest re-collection occurred when I was three years old. It should have been when the story ended.

We were travelling home one summer's evening in my father's old two-door black Austin Seven with its doors that swung out and back. Pre-seat belt era. I can only think that I'd seen my dad opening his door to throw something out, because I distinctly recall doing the same thing. On this occasion I was attempting to fling out my apple *dootsie* when the wind caught the door, pulled it open, and then threw me out and away from the car. My mother screamed as her red-suited son whizzed past the window. I bounced on my head a few times before landing on the road a couple of hundred yards back. When my dad picked me up in his arms I remember looking up at him and asking,

"Will I ever walk again?"

Luckily the traffic back then was slight which is the main reason I did not end up minced meat; it was the first of my many head injuries. People went about things differently then; it was a time when the doctor would come to the house to treat you – but on this occasion we visited him. He was rich and the house was old and large. It must have been close to Christmas as I recall seeing a brand new bike wrapped up in the hallway. *Some kid is a lucky bastard, getting a bike for Christmas,* I thought (I didn't actually think the word bastard, probably more like person or boy; I never swore when I was wee, not even in my head). The doctor put some powder on my noggin and that was it; I was able to run around in circles again.

"Don't fall out of any more cars," was his advice as we were leaving.

Holding my dad's hand I looked back and thought, *OK, I won't you old bastard* (again not the word bastard, more like *OK, I won't you weirdo).* It was a strange bit of advice, as if I fell out of cars once or twice a week.

I was raised on a newly formed council housing estate in North Belfast; it was a completely working class area but with some grass instead of concrete. By the late sixties the complex would grow to become the largest in Europe – we even had a TV documentary about it. Before the Troubles started the area was a relatively safe, fun place for both Catholic and Protestant kids to live and play. At this time the estate had approximately 15,000 people with around a 60%-40% split in favour of the Protestant faith. I can remember being aware that the Catholic kids were different but apart from them attending different schools, not being able to play cricket, their eyes being too close together, and kicking with their left feet, I was not sure just what the difference was. Nowadays it would be quite easy to distinguish a Catholic from a Protestant without directly asking them what their religion was outright. The following are a few simple questions that would reveal their faith.

1. Pronounce the letter H.
2. What is your nationality?
3. What country do you live in?
4. What football team do you hate the most?

Catholics	*Protestants*
1. Haitch	Aitch
2. Irish	British
3. Ireland	Northern Ireland
4. Rangers	Celtic

We were brought up Protestant though my parents never showed any animosity towards the other religion: they had good Catholic friends. One of my aunts on my mother's side had married a left-footer and that had not been an easy decision for either of them to make. It had taken a while before my grandfather and five uncles had accepted him. Both my parents' families lived on the same street, each with 10 kids, and dad's brothers had also given the new groom a wide berth. He was one of my favourite uncles with a sense of humour second to none: always telling jokes and acting the *eejit.* When someone from my family described Jack to people who did not know him they would say:

"Jack's a Fenian like, but he's a really nice fella."

That summed him up; he was in fact a Catholic and a really nice man who liked a drink and kept everyone entertained. I was in my Uncle Jack's house a lot growing up and the first FA Cup final that I remember watching was in 1965 between Liverpool and Leeds whilst sitting on his knee. It was a tedious first 90 minutes but the game burst into action during extra time and looked certain to go to a replay after Billy Bremner had cancelled out Roger Hunt's opening goal for Liverpool with a fine 100th minute equaliser. But the Leeds supporters' hearts were broken when Ian St John scored what turned out to be the winning goal a mere three minutes later.

His wife, my Aunt Lily, was like a second mum to me and her house was my other home with my older cousins Lillian and Kathleen frequently babysitting. They would nip me until I cried then cuddle me to make it better: strange girls but they loved me really. Their brother John C. would take me with him on his travels, sometimes just to sit at the shops watching the cars drive by around the estate as he taught me the names of each model. I remember walking around singing. "Na, na, na, na, na, na, na", doing the grand finale of *Hey Jude.*

Many a time during those early days my aunt would ask my dad to drive into town and collect Jack from one of the many pubs he drank in. By 1974 my uncle and aunt would move to Canada to join their daughters and get away from the sectarian attacks that would drive Catholics out of the estate during the bloody, early days of the Troubles.

Every Saturday my mum took Kathleen and me across town to my grandparents' house to join the throng of cousins that descended on 16 Thornhill Parade near Stormont to disrupt their tranquil settings. Further up the street was my other granny's house and we'd spend time there as well until she died in 1963. Apart from my Uncle Tom the remainder of the 10 kids on my dad's side lived outside Northern Ireland, so there wasn't the vast herd of cousins visiting as in my mother's family. We'd get the blue bus into the town centre then go for something to eat at the Copper Griddle in High Street while waiting for the red bus to take us up the Newtownards Road. I remember sitting in amazement, looking from the café's window and watching the maintenance men attempting to put the large conducting antennae of the trolley bus back onto the overhead wires. They were using a long pole with a hook on the end which they had pulled from a hole in the back of the bus. I thought it looked like great fun and would have loved to have tried using the giant rod to connect it all together again. When our bus was ready to go I would curiously watch with suspicion as my mother always left some pennies under her tea cup saucer before leaving the restaurant. Arriving at my grandparents' we'd sit in the living room at first then gradually begin to cause havoc with my granny pulling each of the cousins to one side to give us a real telling off; my granda didn't care: he loved us having fun. On my mother's side I had 26 cousins and probably half of them were there every Saturday running up and down the street or playing football on the grass in the middle of the parade: bedlam. With his long hair and penny whistle, my Aunt Marion's son and older cousin John H. was like one of the Beatles to us. He lived with my grandparents along with Uncle Robert, and we'd all try and get his attention to play with us or take us down the lane to the sweet shop. Sometimes if we were really lucky we got to go into Mrs. Dunne's house next door to play with her pet monkey, parrot and mina bird. Fantastic days that leave me with beautiful memories.

On my estate we all mixed as children. Religion didn't enter into the equation; we were just innocent kids. My dad and my uncles were all in the Orange

Order and would march in the parade to the Field every 12th of July. A band, usually playing flutes and drums, followed the Orange Lodges, each of which carried a large banner with a mural of the king or queen or a scene from 1690 at the Battle of the Boyne: a battle between a Dutch king and an English king in Ireland. That is when all the trouble started: bloody foreigners, why didn't they find somewhere else for a scrap? The 12th was like going to a carnival for us; everyone was singing and dancing and having fun. The kids had a great day out; we didn't think about the history or religious significance.

When I think back to the early sixties it was as if Northern Ireland was punished for having it too good. We were always happy; being a kid then was great. All my memories from then are fond, golden memories; I always felt secure and loved. The top news headlines from Belfast in those days were so trivial that the focus was on problems across the water. Thinking back on a holiday at my aunt's home in St. Albans, England, I recall that a young girl was murdered close by. It scared my sister and me so much that we slept in our parents' room until we left. I imagined how unsafe it would be to live there. Five years later Belfast erupted and killings would be commonplace with my estate gradually changing to become a dangerous place to live.

Growing up in the sixties was a great adventure. Looking north my new home was greeted by a partial border of open fields and a hill that stretched out into the countryside. The shipyard was the southern view: not so picturesque. This wooded recreational area would be the setting for some of the happiest days of my life. Billy and Brian, my closest friends, were ever-present. From when we were three-years-old until our late teens we were rarely apart, going on holidays together and joining various organizations such as the Scouts and Boys' Brigade. It is sad that our relationship faded since we were so close during our childhood years: years in which we helped one another overcome various difficulties and fears. Gradually we drifted apart, each of us going our own separate way until eventually we lost contact – something I will always regret. We'd see each other occasionally over the years but not nearly enough. Billy got married and asked if I would be best man at the wedding. We were just 18; he was not ready for marriage and I was certainly not ready to be best man. His new bride disliked Brian and me so her influence on Billy was the beginning of the end for the three of us.

Along with some of our next door neighbours, a family of 11 and various other kids from the street, we would spend most of our free time up The Hill, as it was known. There were three long dirt tracks that slithered down through the hill that we called Donkey Slides; god knows where the name came from. The Donkey Slides were the fastest route home and we would all slide down them at the end of the day thus tearing the arse holes out of our jeans, and receiving right old *bollickings* from our mums.

The Hill had many hidden areas of adventure. Our first stop was usually at the Yellow Lorry, an old beat-up and discarded truck that we would climb over and pretend to drive. Then it was on to the Goat's Cave, a small enclosure with a stream that trickled down over its craggy top to a crystal clear pool below. We would pause here and drink thirstily from it before we ventured deeper into woods. This is how I remember it but in reality it was a muddy hole in the hill with a puddle of water beside it. I could not imagine the youth of today being offered a drink from this utopian oasis; it would have to be sterilized, pasteurized, circumcised, bottled and blessed by the pope before they would be able to sample it. Our destination would always be Mackies, an abandoned factory with machinery long since silenced and an assortment of derelict offices to explore. Around the back of the building were several pits that were overgrown with plant life and filled with water, and housing some interesting creatures such as frogs, toads, wildebeest, sticklebacks, lesser spotted things and that elusive salamander: the newt. If you caught a newt you were the *dog's bollocks*; everybody wanted a newt. Mackies had a large brick wall around part of it; it was too high to climb over and an attempt to do so would be futile due to the broken glass cemented into its top. This savage wall-topper was a great deterrent to the would-be burglar or intruder; unfortunately this practice has long since been banned, which is probably why a lot of properties are effortlessly broken into nowadays.

What was actually on the other side of the forbidden barrier caused our curiosity to rise and the challenge was on to unlock the dark secrets beyond. There were always a couple kids who were as daft as a brush and ready to try anything; they were the bad kids, the ones from a family of 10 or more, *boggin'* with snotters tripping them. Their dads were either missing in action or in jail and they washed regularly once a month whether they needed to or not. One of the stories that I believed for years was that there was a band of crazy gypsies that camped against the back of the wall hunting for any unfortunate lost child on their side. After abduction they would be gone forever, brought up as a slave to the gypsy tribe. A small gap – created by a few crumbling bricks and big enough for a good-looking dwarf to look through

– was the only window to the unknown beyond. One of the annoying smelly kids who hung around Mackies would always try to impress us with his endless lies. He shrugged off the scary stories of wild gypsies and claimed that he'd been behind the wall so we called his bluff and dared him to go through. Like a mug he fell for it, cautiously guiding his head and shoulders into the hole before halting; he was beginning to have second thoughts about continuing and was noticeably afraid. Before he could get out we held him in place then pushed him further into the gap, wedging him in so tight he was unable to move. He began to squeal like a stuffed pig as if the devil himself was trying to drag him through. As he resisted he began to blow out loud wet farts, which indicated that there was a possibility of a shite explosion occurring; luckily though he only pissed himself. The echo of his distress calls could be heard for miles so we thought we'd better pull him out but he had squirmed so much trying to free himself that he had become fixed: we could not shift him. No one wanted to get too close considering he smelt like a chimp's arse after a PG Tips tea party. After about 20 minutes of struggling unsuccessfully to free himself he went a blue-grey colour then passed out. It looked like he was dead. Everyone there panicked; some just ran away. Eventually the fire brigade was called to cut him out, causing a great commotion in the area involving the newspapers and a television crew. Billy, Brian and I on the other hand got into big trouble and were banned from going to Mackies for a while. In due course we were freed from our detention and began our adventures up the Hill again.

Close to Mackies was a section cordoned off with the usual Trespassers Will Be Prosecuted sign, which of course everyone totally ignored. There was nothing in this area apart from a strange hole in the ground enclosed within a small wrought iron rail that at first glance seemed to be filled up with tarmac or some other material. Naturally I climbed over the fence and walked across the crusty surface. My feet sunk into the black stuff that held me there like glue and as I attempted to walk away I felt myself slowly descend into the sticky mixture. I grabbed the surrounding railing to prevent myself slipping further into the hole but by then I was stuck waist-deep. Billy and Brian stood motionless watching me as I began to disappear from view before eventually taking action to prevent my imminent demise. They came to the rescue and managed to pull me free of the tar-like quicksand. My new light blue jeans were completely ruined as they were covered in the black, sticky substance and so were my shoes and socks and once again I was in trouble with my mum. We never went near the hole – which we simply called the Black Stuff – again. So just what was that black stuff? Why was it there? Was it a Venus flytrap for kids? Lots of lost souls may still be entombed at the bottom of this sloppy pit playing sticky games together.

Winters were never anything to get excited about apart from the wonderful days of Christmas: magical times from long ago that now seem like one of the festive stories on television. Most children from then will remember with similar fondness: family get-togethers; decorations; turkeys; and what Christmas was really all about – the presents. We didn't get much but I looked forward to a compendium of games, the Beano and Dandy annuals, an apple and an orange and maybe a comb. It was brilliant; what else could you ask for? Anyone in my age bracket will certainly remember the winter of 1963. This was a Canadian-type winter that started in November and lasted until March. It was so bad the football matches were cancelled throughout those months and a panel of experts was needed to forecast the results. People in those days dreamed of striking it rich by marking out eight lucky drawn games on the football pools so it was important to have the panel of experts. Although the long winter starved the people of football a splendid league cup final was contested in the spring between fierce second city rivals Aston Villa and

Birmingham City. In those days it was a two-legged affair and Birmingham City took home advantage with a fine 3-1 win with Jimmy Bloomfield netting a Harris cross to go three up after 66 minutes. A late Thompson strike made it interesting seven minutes from time but Birmingham lifted the cup after the two teams played out a dour goalless draw in the return match at Villa Park.

No one was prepared for such a bad winter; there were not any shovels to remove snow and ice from pathways and the council had few snow ploughs to clear roads. Tripping over the small two-foot walls that surrounded the houses was commonplace as we waded through the snow trying to get to our homes. With this blast of Arctic fun downsides were inevitable, and road accidents were common, particularly one a bit too close to home. My dad owned what was probably the biggest family car that Britain ever produced: the Vauxhall Cresta, a car that would not be out of place in the USA. Shocking pink in colour, it had a bench seat in the front that my cousin John C. and I would occupy when out for a ride, and an enormous bonnet with an upright Vauxhall ensign in the middle. We would watch this ensign like a target as we pretended to steer then straighten the car as it rounded each corner. The size of the car was the major reason my father was not killed that winter. He and a friend were heading out one evening, carefully negotiating the snowy main road that curved through the estate. At one of the many bends an oncoming bus slid over to the wrong side of the road and hit the Cresta head on. The car was wrecked but my dad and his passenger received only minor head injuries. The bus driver was drunk but unhurt. I don't recall what punishment he received: probably not much as drunk driving was not taken as seriously back then as it is now. When the insurance claim came through we got another Vauxhall Cresta, grey this time. There must have been no pink ones left.

Looking back to my early childhood I find it hard to remember being sad at any particular time though there were occasions when I thought hard about death and what it really meant. An eerie experience happened when I was about six years old, just two doors away from me. The family had a new baby to join with a sister and two brothers. He was named Stephen. I don't remember much about the child but I do remember when he died. He could not have been more than three months old and I recall one of the brothers taking me upstairs to the bedroom to show me him lying still on the bed. This frightened me and although puzzled by the circumstances I felt very uneasy being in the room with a dead baby. My memory makes me believe I saw two large copper pennies on the baby's eyes but this might very well be my mind playing tricks. Whatever the case that is how I remember it and I found it hard to get it out of my head. Not quite as bad as the movie *Trainspotting* but I was seeing a dead baby for a while all the same. Soon after he was taken from the house in a tiny white coffin and buried in the cemetery close by.

Another horrific incident shocked everyone in the estate. A toddler was pedaling around on his wee tricycle when it tipped off the path onto the road where new tarmac was being laid. The boy fell off his bike and rolled into the path of a giant road roller; the driver had no chance of seeing the child fall and rolled on, crushing the youngster. Everyone was devastated; how could such an accident happen? A few years later I played on the same football team as the kid's two older brothers. One of them was also to be dead by the age of 18: killed in a road accident whilst in the army. Some families suffer more than others.

Most evenings we would play football in the street then move on to Batman and Robin or Superman, depending on whether or not we could borrow our mum's aprons. If we could, they would tie them carefully to our backs then send us whizzing off into the fray. Saturday nights were always the best: burn yourself out then listen for the call around five o'clock. "Come in, Doctor Who's on!" Then *whoosh* – the street was cleared. Brian called it Doctor *MaWho* and hid behind the sofa until the scary music was over at the beginning of the show. Later we would all walk around outside with house plungers on our outstretched arms saying "I am a darlick, exterminate" – rather than *dalek* – in a voice similar to that of someone who had just drunk a cup of bleach. House plungers were essential items which were used by kids for more than just dalek parts: we stuck them to our faces, on our heads, and anywhere else they'd fit. No wonder we all smelt like shite at the end of the day.

Things I remember fondly from those endless summers which we spent lazing around idly are the distinctive sounds and smells: milk bottles rattling in the early morning as the milk men did their rounds; the bells of the Mr. Whippy ice cream van – or better still, Stewarty inside his wee grey Morris Minor van making big thick *sliders* and *pokes* out of Walls ice cream blocks; the lemonade lorry as it came up the hill each Friday for our weekly: one bottle of brown lemonade and one bottle of white lemonade; and the unmistakable smell of the chip van sending the aroma of salt and vinegar wafting into the air as kids queued for a six penny bag. The smell of the freshly baked bread and cakes from my dad's Tip Top Bakers van still lingers in my nasal cavities, and in my memory I will forever carry the vision of our dog Cheetah – a half greyhound-half boxer – bounding from the house to greet my father; leaping into the air and up through the van's side window; landing on his lap; and then licking him to death. Sadly Cheetah was later taken away from us because the local farmer complained that she was running around worrying his sheep. Apparently the satanic mutt would sneak up behind the poor little ewes and tell them there was no God.

One classic scene from my childhood I recall particularly fondly, although it returns to me at a poor postman's expense. As kids we would pass the day sprawled out on a small patch of grass close to our homes. It was certain that our housing estate had one of the largest dog populations in Western Europe because there was more shit than grass. Everyone had at least one dog and they roamed in packs; the most popular breed as in most working class areas was the *wee brown dog.* The hounds chased anything that moved faster than 10 mph and seemed particularly partial to car wheels as they spun around.

The postman that serviced our streets arrived every day on schedule, with mail sack over his shoulder and riding his bright *Noddy*-like post office moped, which was a 50cc motorbike. On this particular day as we lazed about, the familiar noise of a moped could be heard, struggling as it farted up the small hill at the end of the street. In the distance the yelping of dogs on the run was a distinctive sound. Then over the brow of the hill it came: first a helmet, shaking furiously, then a very disturbed postman with his bike swaying from side to side as he kicked out at the pack of dogs in pursuit. We watched as he passed in front of us, by this time with one dog attached firmly to his leg; then *crash!* – The bike went over and the letters flew into the air. Luckily the dogs were more interested in the mailbag than the postman, although a couple of them did have a go at him on passing. As the postman lay in a heap with his moped tangled and smoking, everyone's mail went into the surrounding fields with the dog pack. We watched this event come to its conclusion but remained in our lazed positions waiting for the next occurrence.

Children played in the street with minimal parental supervision and nothing seemed likely to threaten the tranquillity of the surrounding area but the harmony was interrupted by a couple of events involving one of my family members. I can vaguely remember visiting my grandmother in hospital before she died after a short illness and her death created a problem with my older cousin. His mother had left him just after he was born so he lived in East Belfast with my grandmother who tried to control him while his father – my uncle – was at sea serving with the merchant navy. Between my grandmother's death and his father returning from the navy, my cousin lived for a period of time in a Doctor Bernardo's home. He had stolen money from my grandmother's home in the past and had usually tried to shift the blame onto me so it was no surprise when he stole my mother's purse. I remember my father confronting him after the purse was found in a hedge a few doors down the street; of course he denied the theft. Over the next two weeks he had stabbed a kid in the back demanding money in a sweet shop; then he and another nutter broke into some houses in the street and smashed them up, throwing furniture through the front windows. In one place they ran a live budgie through a mangle. He eventually got caught and was sent to borstal for three years.

We got over the wild antics of my cousin and continued on with the good life. The oldest of my next-door neighbours was a Teddy boy and he'd entertain us singing some Beatles numbers as he slicked back his hair in preparation for a wild date; his younger brothers harmonised in the background. Another of the brothers would sneak up on the kids in the street with his dad's old WW2 gas mask on pretending to be a creature from Doctor Who. Brian ran off sobbing hysterically the first time he came face to face with the gas mask and stayed at home for a couple of days until he was sure it wasn't really a creature from outer space.

My sister Kathleen and I had the usual confrontations and although we got on well together, when she lost it I was in fear of my life: she certainly had a wild temper at times. When she was in one of those moods I stayed well clear of her as she tended to slap me about from time to time. After being seriously wound up by me on one occasion she sliced a hand badly by putting her fist through the window of the glass door that separated the living room from the kitchen. I was holding the door preventing her from getting into the kitchen and could see her mad face through the glass as she tried to get hold of me. Luckily the next-door neighbour heard the commotion and came to the aid of my sister by using her nursing skills to bandage the wound until she was able to get stitched up. This incident could have been a lot worse: I could have had my toes cut off.

CHAPTER 2

Primary School

Five years of fun and laughter had passed then suddenly I was torn from my mother's apron strings and forced to go to school. How could they do this to a young child? I was not ready for this; no one had informed me that I was about to be thrown into a building full of yappy kids wetting themselves and crying for their mammy's all day. The trauma of being enlisted with all the other pocket-sized confused individuals was evident: so many faces of fear as they waved their outstretched arms while watching their mums disappear from view after leaving the secret room. I sat grasping my mother's hand intensely with my eyes fixed on the brown door through which each child was hauled after his or her name was called. My only comfort was that my friend Billy was sat next to me due to the alphabetical arrangements. We had toddled together before progressing to running and jumping together, and in the long run we would be together from our first day of school right through to our last day at grammar school. I don't remember the next week or much else of my initial year at school but that first day is still crystal clear.

My primary schooldays were mainly non-eventful with very little of interest to recollect. The school was a prefabricated building that looked like a temporary structure maybe built from access materials left over from the war. Adjacent to it was an old Nissan hut that my mum would drag me into periodically as I kicked and squealed to get free. This place terrified me, especially the piercing buzzing noises that echoed throughout the tin frame: it was a barber's shop and I hated it. A frightening event occurred during a lunchtime trip over the road from the school to The Candy Shop, remembered as *he andy sho* due to the letters missing form the sign. A few kids and I were waiting to go onto the zebra crossing when a lorry skidded, slammed into a telegraph pole and spun round. The back end of the truck would have knocked us over like skittles if it had not been for the quick thinking of Mr. Stallard, the caretaker and lollipop man, who forced us to the side of the road avoiding a disaster.

One major incident that comes to mind was being sent home one morning because the school had been vandalised: windows smashed; books scattered and torn; and paint poured over the floors and walls. One of the two boys responsible had painted the word *basterds* on one wall and all I could think was, *'They can't even spell!'* I was probably eight or nine years old then and never swore but knew how to spell curse words correctly so these degenerates must have been really dense. The vandals responsible for the mayhem were not friends of mine but both were in the same year in a different class. The most distressing part of all this turmoil was the destruction of the school's new blue and gold football kits which had been soaked with bleach and the sad sight of the smashed fish tank with the lifeless fish strewn on the ground below. Both of the little *basterds* were rounded up and kicked out.

Primary five was a good year and I can recall humbly the prestigious honour of being runner-up in Mrs. McCauley's distinguished poetry contest. A nerd called Gordon won the event and although I thought my work was a masterpiece, his *The Tortoise* was definitely worthy of the grand prize: a Milky Way bar. Each poem had to be about an animal and my submission *Dogs* was a creditable challenger for the award but I had to be content with second place and a custard cream biscuit. I'm sure there were at least two verses but this is all I can remember.

Dogs have hard feet, dogs eat the meat
When the dog lays down its head,
then it's time to go to bed

Gordon's *The Tortoise* also had a dog mentioned in his poem although it was in a bad light, as it tried to eat the tortoise. He was a big drip with an extended chin that was always miles in front of his sluggish body which was held back by big flat feet as he sloped along. He wasn't much of an athlete. I didn't like him much before the contest and ignored him completely after it: I was a real bad loser. His poem went something like:

And the dog closed his mouth and cracked his teeth
Ha, that will teach him to try and bite my underneath

I enjoyed the challenge of Mrs. McCauley's literature tests and decided to try and gain an advantage by cheating in a competition to find the best pun. Instead of submitting one pun I submitted 10 puns to see if one of them would win. But *no pun in ten did*.

At home there was little to do in those days apart from dashing around like headless chickens in the open fields adjacent to our street but that would soon change. Someone decided to bring us a playground: right to our doorstep! Previous plans to build a new main road were to be put into action and with it came all the fun and games any nine year old boy could ask for. The peace and quiet was replaced with chaos: trucks; bulldozers; cranes; JCBs; and the greatest piece of equipment of them all – the scraper – had arrived amongst us. Scrapers were like enormous prehistoric creatures that chewed up the earth as they moved along. Nothing could stop these dazzling yellow beasts; they were magnificent.

We got to know the drivers by name and soon we were up there riding with them, Lords of the Manor, the lot of us. There was nothing like the thrill of feeling the machine cruising effortlessly over the rough terrain, seeing it gouged up into the animal's vast belly, carted off and emptied out, causing a complete transformation of the landscape in front of us. I remember one driver named Pat: everyone wanted on his scraper, not because he was any different than the other operators but because he had no roof on his machine. This was the ultimate ride; as the co-pilot sat proudly, up on high, as the scraper paraded along for all to world to see.

Large hills and craters had been formed from the access dirt that had been scraped and then discarded by the mechanical creatures. During the summer months these muddy earth mounds would be our forts and castles, and so the Donkey

Slides were put on hold for a while. Of course this was Belfast and it rained from time to time so our playground could become quite moist and would be appropriately christened the Muckies. One soft plateau formed by the movement of earth was to become particularly popular. It had a great vantage point due to its elevation, and would for some reason be known as Honolulu, maybe because of the abundant supply of our favourite exotic wild plant, the *sarlick*. What these green leafy roots were was open to debate but we scoffed them by the handful and of course would feel quite sick if we were to overindulge, which of course we did.

One of the neighbours fancied himself as the host of the London Palladium and used Honolulu to stage some of his solo acts or a double act with one of his not too willing sisters. "And now ladies and gentlemen," he would announce: "a big hand for Jacqueline in Blue Jeans" and he'd shove her out into the middle of the imaginary platform, her face beet-red with embarrassment. It is certain his inspiration came from the sixties hit by Mark Wynter, *Venus in Blue Jeans*, and although his effort was not a classic it definitely entertained us. Honolulu was also a good drinking and shagging spot for the older kids – not that we knew anything of that kind of stuff.

One joke the kids loved around this time made me roar with laughter no matter how many times I heard it.

A chief in a Red Indian tribe was having bad pains in his belly because he could not fart and sat in his wigwam groaning. Every so often one of the braves would go into the wigwam to report his condition and he would come back out and say "big chief no fart" then later on "big chief no fart", then later on "big chief no fart", and on, and on. Then suddenly a large bang was heard as the chief flew up through the top of the wigwam. The brave went over, looked inside, came back out and said, "Big fart no chief"

Here are some of my favourite jokes from those days.

Q. *What do you get if you cross a sheep with a kangaroo?*
A. *A wooly jumper*

Q. *What do you get if you cross a sheep with a mouse?*
A. *Big holes in your skirting board.*

Q. *What is black and white and red all over?*
A. *A newspaper*

Q. What is black and white and red and can't turn round in corridors?

A. A nun with a javelin in her back

Q. What is the height of pain?

A. Sliding down a razor blade and using your balls as a brake.

For as long as I can remember we were always telling each other jokes and I think our sense of humour helped us through the troubled times that followed.

Along the construction path large concrete pipes were laid end to end, ready to be dropped into place for the drainage system. This was a perfect above-ground tunnel for us to use to make our way back and forth between our houses, especially when it rained, as we could dart between the great cylinders and dry sanctuary. It was a shame to see them disappear into the man-made channels because it seemed much more practical to have the concrete tubes on top of the ground. One particular pipe was painted yellow; this was our favourite one and we would all crowd into it when it rained singing *'We all live in a yellow submarine.'*

Even though the man-made playground was seasonal, it was just as much fun in the winter. The huge craters created by the construction teams produced miniature lakes during the rainy season – which seemed to be every other day – and skating rinks throughout the colder months. It was on one of these bodies of water that yet another harrowing event of my young life took place. January of that year had been particularly cold, which had caused the ponds to freeze over, but the ice was certainly not thick enough to support herds of little people scurrying across the surface. Five or six of us had gathered in the middle of the pond doing what kids are supposed to do on ice: jump up and down. Then *crack!* – The ominous sound below our feet caused a mass evacuation towards the edges. I scampered along the crackling surface trying to avoid the splintering tentacles which pursued me as if trying to grasp my feet and pull me toward them, but I did not completely make it. Then, *splash!* – I went in, grappling at the muddy bank as the heavy, frigid water dragged me back. I managed to grab hold of a large rock and was able to prevent myself from going directly under, though I was still slowly sliding down and certain to be soon submerged. Throughout the chaos I could hear kids squealing as they cleared the ice and ran off into the sunset but now there was an eerie silence. Looking up I could see only Brian; everyone else had just kept running until they had reached their homes.

"Don't just stand there, Brian, help me!" I cried.

Brian reacted by edging down the bank to grab my arm and halt my slide, although thinking back he may have watched me slip into oblivion if I had not awakened him from his trance. He held me for what seemed like an eternity before my mum along with every kid in the street arrived to pull me from the frozen pit of doom. He had saved my life and I was to return the favour a few years later by pulling him off the train tracks after he'd fallen over running away from an angry crowd we'd upset earlier at a disco. This incident wasn't as much of a near-death moment as my sinking below the ice: mainly because the next train was not scheduled to roll through for another 15 minutes.

Before the construction of the new road began, a small farm had thrived on the edge of the estate where the countryside started and the city ended. The farm owners sold off some of their land to allow the road to be built but still continued to operate as a scaled-down version with one old pig and a grumpy old goat (that might have been the farmer and his wife). With the large flow of workmen and pedestrian traffic passing ever-closer to the farm a wee shop opened selling all sorts of stuff out of a converted stable. What a time you could have there with a shilling: penny chews; midget gems; sports mixtures; fruit salads; and something called a yellow man. These strange rectangle-shaped delights were stored in a jar and I'm sure I can remember that some of them had a hidden *thruppenny* or 3d bit inside. Not a good thing considering you might choke to death if one was to stick in your throat or maybe be poisoned by a chemical reaction from the dirty old brass coin. Some days if you felt extravagant and wanted a real treat the whole shilling could be blown on either a bag of clove rocks, pineapple chunks, pear drops – or if you wanted to be brave, some brandy balls. This little shop of innocence was later to become a club run by one of the paramilitary groups and was the perfect location for the occasional beating or kneecapping to take place.

Playing football at school break or later on in the street was my favourite pastime and in the summer of 1966 the ultimate event was taking place in England: the World Cup Final. On a recent trip back to my roots I walked along the old street that had been filled with young fanatics during that football extravaganza. Upon close inspection of a large rock I could just barely see the remnants of some words which had once been written in white and brown paint. Although unable to read them I vividly remembered a kid called Jimbo daubing "England" and later that evening Billy B. attempting to overwrite it with "West Germany". Homemade banners had been prepared for the parades that had taken place up and down the street with two groups of rival supporters growing larger as the cup final had approached. These rallies had been friendly encounters with little more than boisterous, competitive shouting taking place. At that time I had not had any inkling to the demographics behind the two groups but looking back it had been an obvious trend for the troubled times ahead in Northern Ireland. All the England supporters had been Protestant and the German followers had been Catholic. Rab, one of the German supporters, had lived four doors away and with his two sisters had enjoyed happy carefree times playing games with myself and the other kids in the street. He had been in our house frequently along with my cousin John C. when school had ended as both had attended the same Catholic facility. This exuberant young boy would grow to become one of the most notorious members of the IRA, dying a slow painful death some 15 years later for a cause he fervently believed in.

Our modest little three bedroom home was just the right size for the four of us to sleep comfortably and have the privacy we each required. Then in 1967 Engelbert Humperdinck was singing *There Goes My Everything* and *Please Release Me* and although these sounds were played regularly over the airwaves it didn't really mean much to me

– but before long I was to comprehend the meaning behind the words. A Warrant Officer in the Irish guards had finished his 25 years of active service and was flying into Belfast from West Germany with his family of one wife, one daughter and three sons. This decorated soldier was my uncle and his new barracks were set up in our house, increasing my family from four to ten people in an overnight coup. For nine months we bumped into each other, fought with each other and generally all went mental. Christmas of that year was chaotic and at times rough with my cousin Colin and I getting into a big scrap over some stolen some Lego parts. Everyone agreed that the construction of my new house was much better than his because he hadn't had enough bricks to finish his garage. My house was unceremoniously smashed to pieces when he threw it against my back as I was leaving the room in self-satisfaction of my architectural superiority. A straight red card was merited for the exaggeration during my simulated dive as the Lego dwelling shattered against my body. We eventually became a close happy family when my Uncle Billy, Auntie Ann, and the cousins finally got their own council house close by.

Simple memories of that house include watching my mum roll newspaper pages then fold them together to use as kindling for the fire in order to heat the water tank for our early morning wash. Later at night my sister and I would snuggle on the sofa with my parents in front of the blazing fireplace to watch a film: usually one starring one of my mum's favourite actors, Dana Andrews or Robert Mitchum. Coal particles would break then spark out of the flames and land on the floor to add another burn patch to the surrounding rug. Sometimes flaming meteorites would land on the lazy old dog, who was snoring away and wouldn't move even if on fire: and even then, only if dragged by the back legs. And who could possibly forget the never used brass companion set sitting proudly on the hearth side?

Most young boys in the area including myself were football nuts, and we spent most nights kicking a ball about until it was too dark or playing *keepy uppy* under the street lights. When I was at home I played Subbuteo in my bedroom complete with a pretend league made up of teams that I had invented using players from across the country, right down to their names and numbers. All the scores and goal-scorers from the games as well as league tables were carefully documented with illustrations in an old school exercise book. I along with some of my friends played for an imaginary local club – Abbey Rovers – in front of crowds of over 30,000. My dad bought a trophy that was to become a Subbuteo challenge cup which my mates and I competed for in our different houses throughout the winter months. I never ever won it.

In the real world of football I was lucky that my dad coached and sometimes played for Cliftonville Olympic, a reserve team in the Irish league. I would travel all around Northern Ireland with him helping to put out each player's shirt, shorts and socks in the changing rooms before the game. At half time I looked forward to the team coming in for their cup of tea as I would have a bottle of lemonade waiting for me: it was magic. One of the young goalkeepers was offered a trial at Chelsea, my favourite team growing up, and incredibly my dad and I were invited to go with him to watch a game at Stamford Bridge. We met the Chelsea chairman, Mr. Mears, and my dad asked if it would be possible for me to meet my favourite player and present him with a Cliftonville pennant. He agreed and walked me to the changing room to meet Charlie Cooke before the match against Newcastle. I was trembling as my boyhood hero was about to be introduced. He had a bandage on his hand because of a broken bone he had received the previous week and I was afraid to squeeze it too hard in case it hurt him.

"How are ya doin' son, looking forward to the match?" he asked in his smooth Scottish accent.

I nodded in approval, unable to utter any words as he passed a Chelsea pennant to me and

I offered him the one from Cliftonville with my hands shaking. Just behind where we stood three more players entered the changing room after a workout in the gym: Peter Bonetti, Peter Osgood and Ian Hutchinson. It was the land of fantasy to me. After I had recovered from my unbelievable encounter Mr. Mears showed us to our specially reserved seats where we were able to absorb the atmosphere and listen to the crowd chanting wildly. Chelsea beat Newcastle 1-0 thanks to a splendid right foot volley from all of 20 yards by Keith Weller that left Newcastle goalkeeper Iam McFall grasping helplessly in a despairing dive. The next week I could not wait to go to school to tell everyone of my brilliant experience at Stamford Bridge, but no one believed me. They were jealous and did not want it to be true but it was all exceptionally real to me.

The most memorable games with my dad were the internationals at Windsor Park watching Northern Ireland play in front of 40,000 rabid supporters. These were the big games for the people of Belfast – especially the Home International Championship each year involving England, Scotland and Wales – but there was a special magic of mid-week European games under flood lights. Only three grounds in Northern Ireland were illuminated in those days: Linfield, Glentoran and the very slight glow of Distillerys' lights at the

Grosvenor Road. They were barely bright enough to light up your living room at dinner time and by the time they warmed up the game was over. The first international game I remember was a 2-0 loss in 1966 against England, the newly crowned world champions, when Bobby Moore paraded the trophy around the ground to generous applause. Scotland beat England 3-2 at Wembley the next year to become the first team to win against England since their famous triumph had crowned them world champions. Scotland then claimed to be the new world champions. George Best was the idol of the Belfast people and I had the honour of witnessing him take the Scotland defence apart in 1967 as he won the game almost single-handed setting up Dave Clements' low left foot drive into the bottom corner at the Kop end for a 1-0 victory.

During the summer holidays, almost every other year my parents took Kathleen and me on the long trans-Britain trek starting with a ferry crossing from Larne to Stranraer then down the motorway to various locations in England. One year was an exception though as we headed off to Europe for an extra long drive travelling through Belgium to West Germany to stay with my dad's cousin in a British army base near Hanover. It was really two weeks on an English council estate and I never met a German. The highlight of the trip for me was when

I received a seven-inch long stiletto switchblade knife from my uncle – he had apparently pulled it from a terrorist's back in Aden during the unrest there in the 1950's.

My dad had three sisters that lived in the north of England and one brother in London and my mother had two sisters and a brother living in the south. These fine locations on our travel list were not the kinds of places that would be top European holiday destinations and *God Only Knows* – a hit by the Beach Boys at that time – is the only explanation I can give for why we went there. The first port of call was to my Aunt Margaret's house and this was literally all that was there: a port. Lancaster was a dirty, smelly dock town with absolutely nothing for kids to do. The highlight of this place was watching boats come and go or playing in the dirt with our four cousins while the adults went to the pub. All the cousins were female so Kathleen was OK playing with dolls and other girly things but I was bored stiff. Sometimes we'd take a drive to nearby Morecambe. It was like the land of the living dead but at least there was a beach there and a great amusement park. I especially looked forward to this trip because we would go on board an old replica pirate ship called Moby Dick, which was docked in the harbour. I would imagine I was Blackbeard and I would pretend to slice all my cousins up.

After that we were off to exotic Oldham, the Royton area: a first class dump. My Aunt Clara lived in a maisonette next to some rundown old factories but although this town was even worse than Lancaster I would have much more fun there. At last I had a male cousin, Jimmy, to play with. He was a couple of years older than me and we had a tremendous time playing in the old factories, throwing stones and smashing any remaining windows in the building: great fun. One time my dad, my uncle, Jimmy and I enjoyed a trip to Boundary Park for a football match, then topped the evening off with steak and onion pies which we each washed down with a bottle of coke: a fine night indeed for all concerned. Oldham was now in division four and put up a great performance, outplaying their Welsh visitors and disposing of Newport County 3-0 with two first half goals and one in the second.

After Oldham we'd stop briefly outside a large hotel in Manchester to visit my dad's brother, Uncle David. My sister and I never got to see him and waited in the car with my mum because we were told it would be too busy for all of us to go in. We'd just sit there patiently until my dad returned with our freshly painted *diddy men* gifts that my uncle had made in his hotel room. I believe the small toy figurines were of *Mick the Marmalizer* and *Nigel Ponsonby-Smallpiece* on that occasion. The hotel was actually Strangeways Prison where my uncle was doing a five year stretch.

Our final stop up north was in Leeds to stay with my Aunt Lily and her two daughters. She had a council house with an inter-city train line about 30 feet from the kitchen. Almost every half an hour all the windows in the house vibrated wildly and the dishes rattled in the sink as a high speed 125 mph train whizzed by. My aunt would call us away from the fence when she heard the train approaching, warning us that the force of the rotating wheels could suck us under. We would run up the garden squealing in fear of the large beast eating us up for dinner. That was all the fun Leeds provided. All three of my dad's sisters would eventually seek a better life by emigrating to Portland, Oregon to join a brother and sister who were already there. When he was old enough my cousin Jimmy joined the USAF but as quick as King Louie could swing from tree to tree in *Jungle Book*, he was shipped back to England to his first posting. At least he could speak the language. Two of my six female cousins apparently made a lot of money selling their English type bodies and becoming exotic ladies of the night. With mugs like they had I'm sure they wouldn't have made much during the daylight hours.

After getting used to the northern accents we were on our way down the M1 to expose ourselves to cockney rhyming slang in the aptly named Isle of Dogs region of East London. Uncle Albert was my dad's oldest brother who had done a runner from Belfast when he was 15 for reasons unknown, jumping onto a steam ferry and on his merry way. I never knew his name was Albert until I was an adult; we always called him uncle Dagol, a mysterious name which seemingly no one knew the origin of. He lived in Millwall, one of the roughest areas in London in a second floor flat overlooking the docks. Shadowy people would lurk in hallways waiting for off-guard strangers to enter the complex so that they could sniff them out for rich pickings. Luckily we arrived in an old Triumph Herald and that was enough to convince the would-be hoodlums not to waste any time on us. The most profitable form of income there came by dismantling visitor's cars and selling the parts to the highest bidder. Scruffy little snot-nose ragamuffins would offer to protect your vehicle for a fiver and as soon as your back was turned they'd call the local distributor of dodgy parts and earn another fiver for finder's fees before vanishing into the concrete jungle. We'd always stay for one night and end up down the local boozer watching my aunt get *blootered* during a good old knees up. By the end of the night there would be drunks all over the place singing beside a piano that had been dragged from the pub out onto the street. A quaint little ale house it was, magnificently decorated with blackened windows covered by metal bars preventing unwanted visitors from *nosey-nebbing* or breaking in. All that was missing was an armed guard on the door. The Kray twins would have felt at home there drinking along with a lot of dubious geezers constantly asking, *"aw roight guvna?"* This old gangster's watering hole would later be demolished along with the crime-infested blocks of flats to build a gated luxury condominium complex for rich yuppies. My uncle and the other Eastenders were herded out up to the East Indian dock road area to newly built rows of terraced houses. There was no choice about moving and although the homes might have been new they did not have the character that made up the old Isle of Dogs. The large metal railings and electrified gates protecting the upper class twits meant there was no longer any access to the waterfront for my cousins and friends to swim in the dock.

After that, we were off to the Camberley area, where we would spend one night with my Aunt Ruby and her kids Brian and Roberta then one more at my Uncle Sam's with my cousins Jaqueline and Paul. This was always fun as they lived in a much more cultural part of England. Finally we would stop overnight in St. Albans at my Aunt Mary's where Kathleen and I fed hedgehogs in the garden before heading north the next day. Back in Lancashire my sister and I would finally get to have some real fun in Blackpool and its golden mile. We couldn't wait to go to the pleasure beach and ride the Big Dipper along with everything else this great town had to offer. At the end of the summer the golden mile really lived up to its name: everything was completely lit up, which made it feel like a real fantasy land. I can still remember the smells of Blackpool: fish and chips; candy floss; and the magnificent salty aroma of the sea wafted in by a cool evening breeze. This was a wonderful way to finish off the endless cups of tea and uncomfortable camp beds. Another smell that lingers in my mind is that of hot toasted wheaten bread, which went along well with a couple of boiled eggs served up in a quaint bed and breakfast in Dumfries. This would be the concluding overnight stay before we boarded the ferry en route from Stranraer to Larne and made our way back home to our own wee beds. Another long summer over and we were back to school to talk about our different escapades from the months just gone.

Primary six started well for me as I was chosen to play for the football team and although my teacher Mr. Hutchins was influential in my selection, in the classroom he did me no favours. He was pretty handy with the cane and at 14 stone and six-foot-two a lot of force went into his arm during each swing. There was always a spelling test of twelve questions at the end of the week and if you happened to get less than nine right you would get a heavy whack on the hand for every word misspelled. This method of teaching had been scientifically studied by experts from around the world and had been proven to turn the little munchkins into prolific virtuosos of the English language. Of course they couldn't use their hands anymore. As I look back now, I recall those school memories fondly – well, maybe not the canings. But everything else was pretty great. Sometimes you don't realize how good something is until you have left it behind.

The completion of the new road marked a turning point that seemed to be the end of those carefree days, mainly because of the heavy traffic going past our front door. My parents had been offered a house with a living room and a front sitting room in the middle of the estate: a nice set up compared to most council houses at the top of the estate. But this move broke me up; I did not want to leave my friends behind for I was sure I'd never see them again even though we were only moving less than a mile away. This distance at my age seemed like 100 miles. Brian and Billy's parents would let them go down to see me as long as they were together but it was difficult for me to go up to them alone. Billy and I went to the same school but as Brian did not I would see him less often than before.

Our primary school days were drawing to a close as we prepared to move on to either a secondary or grammar school, depending on how well you could handle the logical Mensa nonsense, the 11 plus. No studying was needed for the grand finale of all exams so all those years of learning did not matter: as long as you could work out that carrto was an anagram of carrot you were laughing. Well maybe not that straightforward but I managed to pass it so that speaks for itself. I believe this test has now been scrapped and something more sensible is being used.

A strange event regarding some council workers and a missing lorry was in the news headlines and caused a bit of a stir in the final year of primary school. We were asked to write a small essay and explain in our own words what we thought had happened. My teacher Mr. McKinnon was not impressed with my account.

The Lorry

One day a big hole appeared in a road near Belfast so the men from the council came out to see what they could do about it. They had a big flat bed lorry and decided to dig the hole up, put it on the back of the lorry then take it away and dump it. They put it on the lorry but when they drove up a steep hill the hole fell off and landed back on the road. They reversed back down the hill to get to the hole but they went too far and the lorry fell into the hole. They were never seen again.

My new house was closer to school so I was able to walk rather than take the bus. Although this meant a bit longer in bed each morning I missed the fun of the bus stop and of racing onto the bus to get the front seats where we would pretend to steer the large double-decker. There were fewer kids playing in the street compared to the old place and things were much quieter: great for my parents but not for me. I did not like it at all.

The school year ended with the 11 plus and I didn't let it worry me too much as I had never expected to pass the exam. A brand new secondary school had been built in the area next to the primary school my sister attended and that seemed to be the natural place to progress to. But to my shock and dismay I passed the 11 plus. This meant I could potentially go to grammar school and this would surely be a disaster living in a working class council estate. It was known as a working class area, which seems strange considering few people actually had a job. The closest grammar school was Belfast High and the pupils there were drawn mainly from the middle and upper classes with possibly 10% coming out of the lower class. Any kids from the area who already attended grammar schools sometimes had to run a gauntlet of abuse on their way home when they got off the bus. It seemed that if you were smart or successful where I lived it was a disadvantage. As the population of the estate increased it brought with it a roughness that had not been there in the early years. Playing an instrument could be trouble for a music geek as they were likely to get their head panned in if they could tinkle the ivories, caress a clarinet or blow out a rendition of 76 trombones.

CHAPTER 3

High School

The opening day at grammar school was like lambs to the slaughter. We were told that all first-years had to wear our caps and scarves to school or we would be expelled; I don't know how we could believe that was enough to warrant an expulsion on the very first day, but we did. The high school was located in a well-to-do area where the dress code was not as intimidating as it was on the estate. Wearing caps and scarves in that area would go virtually unnoticed but it certainly would not where I lived. As we lined up at the bus stop in our immaculate uniforms we were attacked by a pack of vulgarians. They came from the shadows and started slapping us about, tearing off our hats and scarves and running away yelling and waving and holding their trophies aloft as they dispersed into the back streets. This was day one; it was going to be a long first term.

My first year at the new school was a disaster. There was so much that I could not do. Mathematics was 100 times harder and I was forced to try and speak different languages, like French and Latin. It was baffling why they wanted me to learn this prehistoric tongue because as far as I knew there was very little chance of anyone at my school becoming a pope. Physics and chemistry: how was I supposed to learn all that stuff? The teachers had fat bellies, walked about scowling, wore smelly, smoky robes and silly hats called mortarboards – and that was just the women! It would not take long before I was in trouble with the headmaster, a portly balding chappy with a very posh accent that sounded English. He was in fact a local man so well-educated that he had forgotten how to speak like someone from Northern Ireland. I was summoned to his office after being caught letting down the bike tyres of a second-year student who had given me a hard time earlier. Apparently the follically-challenged principal loved to swing the cane so I was thinking of shoving some books down my trousers before my unwelcome meeting with him; I'd seen Winker Watson use this clever ploy in the comics. The plan was scrapped when I was made aware that he would have surely noticed that my arse was a square shape and that this redundant tactic had been tried many times before. Teachers in those days seemed to get sexually aroused by corporal punishment because they were always at it. Most of the classes were boring and the tutors were very strict but we did have history lessons under the loose guidance of Doc Hennesy. He was a dodgy aging cross-eyed *git* with one eye looking at you and the other looking for you. My learned scholar was surely the basis of this classic joke.

> *Hear about the cross-eyed teacher?*
> *He had no control over his pupils.*

He was a part time Baptist minister and may well have been an occasional paedophile although if that were the case one would have thought that the priesthood would have been more his calling. A nice man he might have been but he did not know how to teach or control a class, perhaps because he was daydreaming about diddling children in his spare time. We would sit through his classes trying to learn stuff, but his rambling in a monotone voice about various events from the past was so boring. The class would begin with an inane lecture, *"blah, blah, babble, babble"* and the kids would immediately turn their backs on him and begin to talk to each other, totally ignoring the sermon. All around the class it was bedlam with students doing as they pleased. It did not seem to deter this fine master and he would keep on prattling out the same old crap unaware that no one was paying the slightest attention to what he was saying. It wasn't unusual for a student to ask for a toilet break and not return to class. One sunny day out of utter boredom during a class I decided to climb out of the window and go over to kick a ball about in the playing fields, certain that old man Hennesy would not notice my absence. None of my classmates knew what I was up to so they were quite surprised by my covert manoeuvre and moments later three of them climbed out to join me. We had a game of *keepy uppy* then crawled back through the window before the class ended. He was still waffling on upon our re-entry, totally oblivious to the fact that we had been out and about. Although I thought we had pulled of a famous caper I was unaware that another teacher, Massie Murray, had been laying low outside and had caught the whole operation in the act. When the class ended I was nabbed by a prefect and marched down to the headmaster's office where I sat in silence waiting for my three accomplices to arrive. We all got our arses slapped and a dose of after school detention for a week. The headmaster hated most of the arrivals from my estate as he seemed to think that we lowered the school standards when various dignitaries arrived for inspection. Just because Billy and I formed our own gang and walked about the corridors slapping all the nerds about – it was no grounds to judge a certain sub-group of pupils!

Grammar schools had no football teams so it was rugby or nothing and that was the main reason I would have rather gone to a secondary school: never mind the education. Rugby was a new game to me but I soon began to enjoy it and the absence of football wasn't a bother as I was playing for a team outside school hours. During a practice match the gamesmaster informed me that I had been selected to play for the rugby team on the following Saturday morning. Suddenly there was a problem: although rugby was enjoyable I did not like it that much. Five days of school activities was enough for me and besides, football was my game at the weekends. After refusing to play I was ordered to the headmaster's office where he threatened me with detention if I didn't turn out for the *rugger* team. This was a dilemma: my love of football was sure to get me anally punished if I did not bow down to my illustrious master and play rugby. After discussing the situation with my dad he decided to go to the school the next day for a meeting with the rotund balding principal. He explained politely that the school could stick the rugby team up their arse because as far as he was concerned the school timetable did not include Saturdays. That was the end of the rugby team for me and although I was still able to play inter-house rugby and any midweek matches I did not play any Saturday games against other schools and thus avoided the usual pasting which we always received from the superior grammar schools, because we were crap. If it hadn't been for Ballyclare HS being so pathetic we would not have won any games. Unfortunately this little episode made me a marked man for the teaching staff to hand out their chosen punishment whenever it suited them.

Billy and I had been in the same class since our first day at primary school so we were always together and after school we'd meet with Brian and hang around for the rest of the night. My mum called us the Three Stooges. Any activities outside school would see the three of us involved. Brian had talked us into joining the scouts and although the thought of running around with a neck scarf and woggle did not appeal to me much we all loved the adventures. During our first year the scout troop took us on a two week camping holiday to a massive jamboree in a place called Buckmore Park in Kent along with scouts from all over Britain. They'd laugh at our funny accents at the camp tuck shop and were a bit baffled why one of us being so young should have a sexually transmitted disease. It all stemmed from overhearing a conversation between Brian and Billy and their pronunciation of a certain word. As they approached the counter Billy asked Brian if he still had *thee D* or as the English would say three D: three pence (3D) in the old pounds, shillings and pence system (LSD). Of course the cloth eared buffoons thought that the poor little Belfast scamp had VD.

At the end of the trip we spent the last weekend in London at Baden Powell House visiting the nearby natural history and science museums on Friday. The next day was too good to be true: we all had tickets for the Chelsea-Manchester United game with over 50,000 people packed into Stamford Bridge. Unfortunately Chelsea lost 3-2 even though George Best was sent off in the tunnel at half time for flinging some unsuitable verbal masonry at the referee. Bobby Charlton scored a fantastic third goal against the run of play and although Chelsea had all of the play they could not force an equaliser. Later that evening we went to see *Kelly's Heroes* in Leicester Square then back to Baden Powell House for a teeny bop disco made up of boy scouts and girl guides. Before heading back home I had just enough money left to buy a couple of singles, *Moon Shadow* by Cat Stevens and *In my Own Time* by Family. We took this great holiday for granted but it must have cost our parents a fortune considering they did not have much money.

Not long after being established as wolf pack squad members our scout leader recommended we should try to win our orienteering badges. After an evening of learning how to read an ordinance survey map and use a compass we embarked on a weekend trek across the glens of Antrim. We were to cook our own food and spend two nights camping along the way: no problem to seasoned survivalists like ourselves. Equipped with tent and provisions we were dropped off at the coastal town of Carnlough. That night we found a field to pitch the tent and prepare our first feast: wondermash potatoes and loads of baked beans; this cooking lark seemed to be easy. An early morning wake-up call from a herd of cattle was unexpected and stepping in cows' shite in bare feet was not much fun either; country living did not agree with us at all. An irate farmer began waving his fists and swearing at us in some strange Scottish-like accent so we didn't hang around long as it was obvious he wasn't inviting us for breakfast.

Smelling like a barnyard we headed toward the glens guided by the craggy peak of Cleggan Forest. The weather wasn't bad for the end of May considering the area was usually cooled by a stiff breeze coming off the Irish Sea. Brian was moaning and groaning: about why he had to carry the tent; that his feet were sore; and that he was starving even though we had walked for not more than an hour. Billy and I were keen to get off the road and onto the glen before the weather changed as the sky was now covered in dark clouds. Brian collapsed by a soft roadside verge yapping and complaining that he could walk no further as the two of us hurried on leaving him sprawled out in the grass.

"Come on ya whimp ye," we shouted as we ignored his plight and continued on without him. Later a tractor pulling a large trailer blew its horn for us to clear the small dirt road so we moved aside to let the red beast by. As it ambled past Brian was lying defiantly on the back of the trailer with two fingers raised grinning widely. The trailer carried on for about 100 yards before the driver was requested to stop by his smug passenger to allow us to board. The farmer took us a few miles along the road to his farm at the base of the glens and though not what our scout leader would have expected, it was better than walking.

A few hours later we were further into the hills and decided to look for a suitable location to pitch the tent and set up camp. Up ahead was what looked like a derelict old house so that seemed like the perfect spot. We forced our way in through the buckled front door of the single-roomed building to find some bedding and empty beer bottles scattered on the floor. The place looked as if it someone had been staying there as the fire grate had remnants of materials that had recently been burned. The only other furnishings in the room were a table with three wonky chairs and a large wooden cupboard in one corner. Upon opening the cupboard doors we found bags of fertilizer, some metal containers filled with nails, and on a shelf below, a notepad with information about army and police activities. Some of the writing was in a different language that we assumed was Gaelic; then it suddenly dawned on us what was going on in the building.

"This place is being used by the IRA, let's get out of here!" I yelled.

Within seconds we were out through the front door and began running back into the hillside, not stopping until the building was out of sight. It was dark before we found an appropriate place to put up the tent and our hearts were still pounding as we discussed what we had just discovered. The next morning we broke camp and hiked close to the peak that had been the halfway point of our trek. By the time we rounded the summit the rain had started to fall and the sky was completely covered with black cloud extinguishing what little light there was. Later we sheltered under some trees to avoid the rain that was becoming ever heavier and after an hour or so the bad weather broke slightly.

"Let's go, it's eased off a bit," said Brian. "The sooner we're aff this hill the better!"

We agreed then packed up our stuff, ready to brave the elements. After a short distance the wind grew stronger and the rain was now relentless; our visibility was limited as we marched completely drenched through the knee high grass. Our enthusiasm for the hike took a severe blow when Billy looked up in despair and said:

"There's that peak again, we're going round in circles!" He was right; we were lost! I suggested that we put up the tent to protect us from the constant driving rain and at least have a temporary respite.

"Good idea," Brian replied, "Then we can check where we are with the compass and map." We struggled with the three-man tent but eventually it was erected and one by one we crawled in through the front flaps to take shelter. The tent was not quite tall enough for us to stand up inside so we knelt down and opened up the map. I put the compass onto the map and asked:

"OK how do we read this thing?" Billy had a big dumb look on his face and Brian's was even dumber. They both had no idea how to read it.

"I thought you understood how to do this after the training session?" I said. It was obvious no one had been listening during our tutorial, with each of us thinking that the other two would take in all the information required to prevent us from wandering aimlessly across the glens. We started yapping and bickering about what our next move would be when suddenly the tent was ripped from its moorings with an extreme gale force blast of wind. The poles spiralled out of control, rattling against our heads as the tent went airborne and within seconds it was gone out of sight. Like deer caught in headlights we gaped at each other as we huddled tent less and took the monsoon in full force. Before anyone could react the map was torn from my hands and went on its way chasing the tent.

"Let's keep walking, we can't just stand here," said Billy. We grabbed our wet packs and trundled on across the glen in no particular direction and it didn't take long before we were back around the peak again to the same spot. We were still going round in a circle. To make things worse a mist had joined the incessant rainfall, which meant we could no longer see the peak, and the peak was an important factor in determining whether or not we were still lost. It was then that Brian fell down on to the ground to shout reassuringly:

"We're going to die out here; we'll never find our way off the glens!"

Billy and I looked at each other and just shrugged our shoulders. I thought that Brian may be right as it would soon be dark, and then we would be in deep doo doo, but I also thought it was better to die trying to get off them than to just give up. We dragged Brian to his feet kicking and screaming then carried on walking until eventually we heard something from above the cloud.

"*Listen! What's that noise?*" Billy asked excitedly, pointing upwards. A helicopter flew overhead, probably on the lookout for criminal activities but we were convinced they had sent a search party out; unfortunately they could not see us and we could not see them, so we were still lost. On and on we struggled, so wet we could feel the water squelching in our boots. *It's every man for himself,* I thought. *Survival of the fittest.* Hunger pains gripped our stomachs as we believed it could be death by starvation. The only remaining items of food were five chocolate penguin biscuits which I had secretly stashed away in my backpack; as three into five was uneven I thought I should eat two of them then offer the rest up as one each. I could have been really greedy and gobbled up the lot, but these were my best friends after all. So I ran further ahead and quickly munched down two delicious penguins. I awaited their arrival then offered up the last of our rations: they could not believe that their best friend had saved the chocolate treats for them.

Our ordeal came to an end when we were halted by a mesh fence. If it hadn't been for the fence we would have walked right off a cliff face which was invisible as a result of the misty shroud that hovered on the glens. We decided to follow the fence and it took us through a path over a mile in length and ended at the most welcome sight of a dimly lit farmhouse. A new surge of energy gripped us as we ran to the door and began banging the large brass knocker with formidable anticipation. An elderly couple cautiously peered through one of the curtained windows before allowing us entry into their modest home. The living room was rather small and was heated by a glorious raging fire that we rushed to with a feeling of great relief. The farmer's wife gathered our wet clothing and offered us warm blankets to wrap ourselves in as we huddled around the blazing fireplace. After explaining our predicament to the farmer he drove off to a general store a few miles away to call our worried parents to let them know we were safe. The old couple had lived in the farmhouse for years and had never had a phone installed. While he was gone his wife fed us with a delicious feast of *eggy in the cup* and loads of toast. It wouldn't be long before we were reunited with our anxious families and sent straight into hot bubbly baths. This tale had a happy ending: we did not perish on the moors. The glens of Antrim had been no match for three seasoned mountaineers.

Our friendship never wavered; even in extreme circumstances we were united. Never was there an instance of malice or conflict between either one of us nor did we ever take sides during minor arguments: for over 18 years we were close, great friends. Although we might have been at each others throats when we were lost on the glens it didn't deter us from further escapades. Over the next few summers we would haul our packs and tents together on trips to the Isle of Man and the Lake District, as well as some of the finer spots in Northern Ireland. But these would be the last of our carefree ventures together. Dark clouds were on the horizon and the innocence of our youth was about to be lost forever as the landscape of Ulster became unrecognisable.

PART TWO

CHAPTER 4

The Dark Days

It would be pointless to discuss the reasons each side wanted to fight and what they were willing to die for during the Troubles but one thing was certain: it was a tragedy. My feelings about the endless conflict have gradually changed the longer that I have lived away from Northern Ireland. At 17 I was an extremely bitter and angry young man very close to ruining not only my life but also the lives of those close to me. I had foolishly considered getting involved with some dangerous people in the fight for the glorious cause but a weekend in Manchester turned out to be the lucky break that prevented me heading to certain heartache. Thinking back on that time it is difficult to believe I could have been that way. Later, while living in England I would try to educate the locals about the struggle in Ulster and the difference between Catholics and Protestants, but to the English we were all the same: *thick paddies*. I quickly learnt not to bother indulging in such conversations; besides it was the only subject that really made me angry so it was better to leave it behind.

At the beginning of the 1960's the economy in Northern Ireland was reasonably strong with the mainly Protestant shipyard in particular thriving, but by 1968 republicanism was also growing: the civil rights movement for Catholic equality was on the march. The early sixties had seen movement out of the traditional religious strongholds of the Protestant Shankill Road and the Catholic Falls Road to surrounding overspills such as my housing estate. By the end of the decade most of the unrest focused on the working class section of Belfast. It was these areas that became the brunt of sectarian attacks with the majority targeting the minority. Usually the families were *burnt out*. Vigilantes took to the streets and before long guns were readily available.

The Troubles slowly infected the province. I was not yet a teenager and was unaware of what exactly was happening as I watched news broadcasts from Londonderry at the end of the 1960's. Hundreds of protesters were clashing with the police and I remember the water cannons hosing them down and seeing them scarper; it looked like fun. But of course it wasn't: this was the start of a desperate 30 years in Ulster's history. The Troubles really took off in 1969 around the same time that Neil Armstrong had shoved Buzz Aldrin out of the way to become the first man on the moon.

Black and white television did not really do justice to the blood spilled by a rioter's brick or from a police baton to somebody's head. One version of the hosing was quite clever: add purple dye to the water, soak the unruly mob, then go back the next day and arrest the purple people. Unfortunately this cunning plan was ineffective as being purple did not mean you had broken the law so anyone arrested was quickly released. I'm sure the purple people would have been discriminated against for being different to the white folk. There was unrest in Derry, so what? It might as well have been in the Congo to me. Londonderry was at the other end of Northern Ireland and not many people from Belfast ever went there. When the army was sent in it was like watching an old war movie. There were troops on the streets but they were not acting: this was real and was soon to be on our own doorstep. The soldiers were there originally to protect the Catholics from the Protestant threat but that soon changed when the IRA raised its sinister head. 1970 had not started so well and the civil unrest took up most of the country's news headlines, which unfortunately meant that a little good news went virtually unnoticed in some areas. After a period of bad beatings and becoming almost 2nd class citizens, in October Glasgow Rangers finally put a halt to Celtic's dominance with a 1-0 victory at Hampden Park in the league cup final thanks to a goal from 16 year old Derek Johnstone.

My first experience of a shootout resulted in paranoia, squeaky bum time, and freezing with fear as people all around me began running for cover: it was mayhem. I'd been to the main library in the city centre and was on my way to the bus station. I was about 13 at the time and the *crack! crack!* of gunfire was very familiar as it could be heard most nights. Instincts tell you to take cover but this was a busy city street and my instincts were to panic – and I did. If they had been handing out panic medals I would have won the gold. The gunfire was apparent but its location was unknown so in a blind fury I ran into the sights of the shooter: a sniper on a rooftop. That was the moment when the *complete life story bit* whizzed through my mind as I gasped for breath. The song *When I'm Dead and Gone* by McGuinness Flint was a chart success then and seemed to be playing in my head. A bus slowed to a half-stop close to me so I threw myself at the door as it accelerated away from the gunfire. The stressed out driver at the wheel was in no mood to hang around and he peeled away quickly. After a half an hour or so I realised that the bus was southbound when I should have been heading north, but at that time a southerly direction was fine with me. Luckily for the intended army foot patrol the sniper was off target: no soldiers were shot and the shooter got away. I was the only casualty – or at least my underpants were.

1972 was to be the worst year of the Troubles starting with 13 people being killed in early January in Londonderry on Bloody Sunday by some soldiers of the paratroop regiment. This event created a large influx of IRA volunteers and brought the main conflict to the streets of Belfast. The sounds of bombs and gunfire would soon become a constant presence and would awaken me from my sleep almost every single night. A lot of families suffered some sort of trauma during these dark days and the first of ours came during this bloody year. I'd just finished kicking a ball about with some friends at the garages near my house when I saw my mum and aunt on the front doorstep of my house crying. I ran up to them to find that my uncle had been shot through the neck and was in hospital, possibly paralyzed. He lived up the Shankill Road and had run out to get his daughter off the street during a gun battle between the IRA and the army. During the chaos rioting had started with both sides hurling bricks and bottles at each other and my uncle had thought he had been hit by one of those missiles. He had held his hand to his neck then had collapsed – a bullet from the crossfire had gone straight through his throat. He had been carried to a nearby car and raced to the hospital. After awakening from surgery he found out that a full recovery was possible although he had been just millimeters from death. He was to die some years later from motor neuron disease; maybe this event had something to do with his illness. I remember being very angry after he was shot, mainly because of the pain it had caused my mother.

The hatred towards the IRA in Protestant areas was growing rapidly. Their indiscriminate attacks became more frequent and unfortunately Protestant retaliation was usually on innocent Catholics. In July of that year Bloody Friday occurred with over 20 bombs exploding in the Belfast city centre, causing death and destruction. There was panic and fear everywhere as we could hear the bombs exploding one by one and waited to hear if my mum was safe: she had been shopping in town that day. Luckily she was unharmed but for other families it would be heartbreak. As this and other events took place I could feel myself getting more and more hostile; the divide in Northern Ireland was widening. With the emergence of the provisional IRA (the Provos), the UDA was forming quickly in large numbers with a promise to save Ulster from the Republican threat. Initially the idea of this force seemed good but it attracted a lot of crazy people willing to do unpleasant things.

The UDA arrived after panic hit the streets and a vigilante force was established with adult men volunteering to protect the housing estate by patrolling at night, usually armed with big sticks. We would be encouraged to gather at the football pitches and learn unarmed combat from a group of semi-uniformed instructors who had little or no training in what they attempted to teach us. But we didn't care. I was 14 and ready for the challenge. Unfortunately so were a lot of other kids and the 16-to-17-year-olds were ripe pickings for UDA recruitment and would usually be in jail within a few months of joining. They were keen to get in on the action, rob a bank or blow someone away for 20 or 30 quid: a lot of money to a teenager considering an apprentice took home about six pounds a week. Refusal to carry out the deed was not an option as the end result could easily be a visit to the hospital for a new pair of kneecaps. Punishment for non-conformists was decided in a kangaroo court with the verdict normally a guilty one. The thought of being summoned to one of these back street trials definitely helped keep vandalism in the area limited. I remember posters going up explaining that anyone damaging or defacing property on the estate would be dealt with. Some ignored the warnings and were soon without kneecaps. The distinct sound of a firearm being discharged could be heard on various nights as some poor soul was on the wrong end of a paramilitary verdict. No one was afraid of the police or army but they were shit scared of internal justice.

By the end of 1972 the city was in turmoil. Army and police patrols were everywhere as violent incidents increased. I'd lie in bed at night and listen to the gunfire and explosions that had concerned me at first but which had gradually become commonplace. One early morning an enormous explosion lit up the sky as if the sun had risen and awakened the community from its slumber. Two IRA bombers had decided to blow up part of the gas works, apparently targeting one of the enormous cylinders. This went somewhat awry as the bomb detonated before they left the scene: something that usually ends a terrorist's employment. The next day a complete section of the Markets Area was gone and all that was left of the bombers were a couple of front teeth and a few pieces of skin. Luckily most of the houses in this area were derelict; otherwise fatalities would have been considerable. The news report informed us that the large explosion in the

Markets had caused 500,000 pounds worth of improvements.

The situation in Belfast was very uneasy. Large groups of Protestants that had been driven out of Catholic areas in the inner city were gradually settling in our area. It was also the beginning of a campaign to drive Catholics out of the estate: masked youths roamed the streets instigating a mass burnout. Protestant and Catholic kids who had grown up together were divided and suddenly we had the highest intimidation rate in Northern Ireland. The terror brigades were by no means inconsiderate; they were actually decent people and would paint a large X on the targeted front doors in order to warn inhabitants of the imminent burn out. Then they petrol bombed the house. Before it was over smoke would fill the sky for a further two weeks until they drove nearly all the Catholic families out. Soon Belfast would produce no-go areas as the working class created segregated ghettos that were either Catholic or Protestant. Most of the middle and upper class areas would go virtually untouched during the Troubles.

My mother's family originally came from the notorious Shankill Road; eventually they moved over to East Belfast but they left a large extended family in that area. One of her cousins, was renowned on the Shankill for being a comedian: always joking around, everybody loved him. One busy Saturday afternoon he was killed in a bar explosion along with another man; he was to be the first of three relatives murdered during the Troubles. The funeral was enormous with both coffins merging half way along the Shankill road: there must have been at least 50,000 people there; it was powerful. As a result of this atrocity some of the family began to seek retribution almost immediately. One of the sons cracked up completely after his dad's death and murdered a Catholic in a frenzied rage of retaliation for the bombing. He was on the run for quite a while and became more and more unstable, committing vicious attacks on his unsuspecting prey. Eventually the police caught up with him; he was later sentenced to life in prison without any chance of parole.

As the destructive events unfolded in Northern Ireland our way of life changed. Belfast was now a segregated city and within these sectors gangs were steadily being formed. At that time I was not quite old enough to get involved in the mob activities but was aware that certain parts of the town were too dangerous to be in alone. Being part of a gang made the individual feel like a hard man; it was easy to be influenced by the groups of youths loitering around doing nothing but inviting trouble. We wanted no part of this. Billy and I spent all day together at school and would meet Brian in the afternoon: he had not passed his 11 pIus exam, the required standard to achieve a grammar school education. Most everyone else from the estate attended the local secondary school so Billy and I began hanging around with a few of Brian's friends, most of whom I'd known from primary school. These were all good lads and a bit more intelligent than the average waster on the street. Our grammar school pals were from different areas so we did not see much of them after the day was done, and besides that they were different: middle class. They did not venture into our estate often.

Football was our connection and the Boys Brigade (BB) had a great league so about 10 of us joined up; it was safer than the UDA. Most of the team were the mates I'd hung around with so the *craic* was great. The league played in and around the Belfast area but the challenge cup was open to all comers throughout Northern Ireland. Our first game was an away trip to Londonderry, a place we'd known only from televised rioting. It was great, all of us crammed into a minibus for a trek across the country to a city most of us had never seen. On our way there we stopped on the Glenshane Pass for a break and instantly began running around the glens like wild horses full of endless youthful energy. We expected a tough match as we were knackered from the travelling but it was no problem: an 8-1 victory. This was the beginning of a very successful team. On the way home we were banging on the van roof singing a variation of *Knock Three Times* by Dawn, re-living each goal that had gone in. Our next cup game was at home against a team from Ballymena and again we won easily; this was perhaps my best ever game. The score was 6-0 and I got four of the goals. Using the advantage of a strong wind I scored two directly from corners, one with my left foot and one with my right foot. My dad's coaching and insistence that I practice kicking with both feet paid off for me that day.

As if I didn't have enough cousins already yet another one came along. My aunt Marion – my mother's sister – and my Uncle Tom – my dad's brother – had been seeing each other for a while and finally got married. Then in 1971 a little cousin – Thomas – came along. With the gene pool mixture being exactly the same I expected a perfect little baby much like myself but this was not the case as the little bundle of joy never stopped crying for months. Then disaster struck in May the next year. My mum and my aunt decided to go shopping and dumped the wee scamp on my lap for the day. Arsenal had picked up the league and cup double the previous year and had a chance to retain the FA Cup against high-flying Leeds United in the final. I know that *sniffer* Clarke headed in the only goal to give Leeds their first ever cup triumph off a Mick Jones cross after he had bravely continued playing with a heavily strapped dislocated shoulder. My problem with this cup final was that I could not hear or concentrate on it because of the constant *gurning* and yapping in the background of my newest relative. This match will always be remembered as the Thomas Croft cup final.

We kept out of trouble playing in the BB league but it was not the same for another local team and although the rivalry between us was intense most of their players were also good friends of ours. Three members of this team would end up in the paramilitaries and ultimately in jail: two of them for armed robbery and one of them got life for murdering a Catholic lad who once had lived close by. They were normal kids from decent families driven to commit crimes that were beyond comprehension. It was difficult to understand why a handful of my friends were slowly distancing themselves and sinking into an evil underworld which was destroying their lives. Regrettably these dark ominous times brainwashed the well-brought-up into committing immoral acts. Two more friends were put inside for six years each after they along with another unfortunate teenager were sent to rob a bank near the shipyard. One sat in the car as the getaway driver and the others went in to grab the cash. They sped off from the scene straight into an army checkpoint about half a mile up the road: caught after only a few minutes – enough time to ruin their lives. The sad fact was that some of these kids could have gone all the way to football stardom: in fact one of their teammates did make it eventually, playing for both Manchester United and Northern Ireland.

Each area began forming its own *tartan gang* and was keen to recruit as many people as possible in an effort to become the hardest and most formidable crew in Belfast. The Woodstock tartan from East Belfast soon became infamous for their daring attacks on other gangs and even managed to get a TV documentary about their exploits. Being in the city centre with tartan colours on was an invite for a ruck so no one went into town alone. Street fights were common, and influenced a lot of ordinary law-abiding citizens to stay away from shopping on Saturdays as the gangs roamed in packs ready for combat. Most of the fighting was Protestant against Protestant so the religious factor was not an issue: the scrap was. The demise of the tartan gangs started when the Bay City Rollers band started prancing about singing *Shang a Lang* with little bits of tartan tied to their shirts. No sophisticated gang member wanted to be associated with the musically challenged *teeny bop* sensations and the squealing

11 year old girls that idolized them. Fortunately my immediate friends seemed pretty stable and our gang activity was limited to a few skirmishes. We went about our lives without getting seriously involved in the escalating situation. Our music taste was also on a higher cultural level.

During all this mob commotion a group of six fruitcakes would go around the estate beating up unsuspecting youths for no reason other than that they were vulnerable or they weren't known to them. They were all skinheads on the shortish side and had a very hard man *dander* that could be heard before they were seen due to the clicking sound of the metal Blakeys on the back of their DM heels. I knew them from school and knew that they were the kind of kids to steer clear of as they would certainly become more unstable because of the lack of brain activity. One fine day Willie and I sat on his garden wall listening to the very fitting *Crazy Horses* by the Osmonds on his newly purchased cassette-radio player when we heard *click, click, click, click* from not too far away; then they turned the corner to where we sat. Shaved bony heads straining forward from their denim jackets like turtle necks from shells they menaced towards us swaying in unison from side to side, the *dander* becoming more pronounced once they saw us. Their leader, completely *radio* (*radio rental...mental*), was out in front, lower jaw hanging open, the few teeth he had left exposed and gnashing. He looked like a demented pit-bull in search of a poodle. As they clumped past Willie said, *"all right boys,"* and with that the maniacal front man swung his head around and into Willie's nose, cracking it open and sending him flying off the wall into the garden below. Without breaking stride they clumped on by without batting an eyelid or speaking a word. I watched as they disappeared out of sight then went to Willie's aid as he lay on his back, stunned, like a dead ant.

Billy and Brian had each acquired themselves a girlfriend so I was not with them every day as I was when we were younger – and Billy's girl was trying to make sure it stayed that way. It was about that time alcohol was beginning to play an influential role in the proceedings. Most of us were about 15 and if you had any type of stubble on your chin then it was easy to purchase some good or bad cheap wine. I first exposed my palate to *devil's brew* in August 1972 at the seaside town of Millisle. It was a place that most of us went to for some part of the summer as either one of your relations had a caravan there or you knew someone else that did. Brian was staying at Billy's family caravan and me with my uncle and aunt. I remember sitting on the wall at the beach watching the world go by listening to *Sylvia's Mother* by Doctor Hook which was playing on a nearby radio when a lad called Ian from my street stopped and sat beside me. It was not unusual to bump into people you knew but when Ian asked me if I'd like a beer I was taken aback. He was a quiet kid and didn't have much to do with the in crowd but as he thought of me as one of the in crowd I had to pretend that I was a seasoned drinker and that I would love to partake in a cool beverage with him. We went to the car park where he opened the boot of his dad's Austin Cambridge and offered me my first ever beer: a bottle of Tuborg Gold. He whipped the top off a couple and handed me one then began swigging his back. I looked at him and thought that I'd better do the same or my lack of coolness would soon be spread about so I did as he did and knocked it back down into my neck. The cool experience of the first beer quenching my thirst on this hot summer's day was abruptly snuffed when I almost spewed it up. I had just partially consumed a heated bottle of undrinkable lager that had been in the car boot for about a week and that tasted like vomit. Trying to keep this disgusting liquid down was a real challenge but I glanced at Ian who was oblivious to my struggle and I managed to compose myself without him noticing that I was really a wimp.

"Thanks Ian, that was great but I've got to go now." I was just able to speak without gagging and coughing everything back up all over him; then

I walked off holding the beer like *Jack the Lad.* He never moved or said a word: I expect he was honoured to be drinking with someone he looked up to. There was still half a bottle left of this poison but when I was out of sight it went straight into the nearest bin. This was a disaster: beer tasted really bad, I thought. How was I supposed to start liking it? After all there would be a lot of drinking to do in the near future.

Millisle was always a fun place to be in the summer but as we got older our pleasure-seeking activities started to differ as we changed from young boys to curious youths. Alice Cooper was at number one with *School's Out*, an anthem that made us look forward to the next year when we would be free at last from the tedious education system. I seemed to be a bit behind everyone else as far as girls were concerned: I always felt intimidated and nervous around them and usually acted like a village idiot when I was in conversation with the opposite sex. But as luck would have it, beer was not to be the only first for me that year.

Most of my education about the *birds and the bees* came from the street, not all of it 100% correct, and as a result I occasionally misunderstood some of the finer things. Learning about when a female had her period was a difficult one for me. Firstly I had to be reassured that if she was on her menstrual cycle going to school she certainly was not riding a bike. In local speak when a girl was having a period it was known as being *on her bad week* and me being so naive I thought that it only happened once in her lifetime. This was evident when I asked Jennifer – a girl from the next street that I'd fancied for a while – to go with me to the cinema. I was astonished that she said yes then my lack of sexual tact became obvious when I began pawing at her like a rabid dog as soon as we got to our seats. She seemed to be enjoying the film and was aware that I was now frothing at the mouth as I tried to slip a hand up her skirt. She slapped me on the wrist to stop my eager fingers climbing towards the Promised Land and informed me that she was on her bad week. *Just my luck*, I thought. *It's a miracle that she agreed to go out with me in the first place then of all the weeks in her life I happen to be with her on her bad week*. Like a mug I found out about menstrual cycles soon after that to a lot of ridicule from my snickering peers – but then no one ever got a diploma from street education.

Back at the caravan site, Patricia, a local girl who had caught my eye, had relatives staying in the same park close to my uncle. She made me feel at ease with her impressive knowledge of the Chelsea team that had won the FA Cup in 1970 and more recently the European Cup Winner's Cup with a fine 2-1 victory over Real Madrid: John Hollins in particular having had an excellent game. We saw each other 3 or 4 times that week and apart from a bit of kissing and cuddling and fiddling about nothing much happened but on the last day I got lucky. She told me her parents were away for the day so I was invited back to her house where she asked if I'd like her to make me happy. She removed her *Magic Roundabout* cardigan and cast it onto the settee. Excitedly I sat in the living room waiting for her to call me and when summoned I dashed to the kitchen where I could not believe my eyes. She was standing suggestively against the table; then with one of her long slender fingers she pointed to a big plate of beans on toast with a sausage on the side and a glass of brown lemonade. It was magic; you couldn't beat it with a big stick. So I filled my face and never saw her again.

By the time of my next trip to Millisle I was prepared for my first full sexual encounter. The lucky lady was in fact a bit of a slapper that was always sniffing around anything in trousers that came close to her caravan and trying to entice them into her web. I'm sure she'd attempted to ensnare someone else before I was caught in her net that day because she was rampant. I smiled upon nearing her caravan and she joined me in a stroll then put her hand in mine; it lifted my self-esteem and I thought that I must be some type of stud to pull a girl that easily. We ended up in the grounds of a borstal that was across the road from the caravan site. She lay down in the grass behind a small brick wall and began to disrobe then said *"Come on."* I looked behind me thinking there was someone else waiting to climb on but I was the chosen one so I approached trembling with fear and mounted her. With a few pointers from her I was able to successfully do the deed although it was all over in a couple of strokes. I pulled up my jeans and was off across the field like the Roadrunner, beeping in delight and leaving her lying there legs akimbo with a look of bewilderment on her face. There were rumours that she would later take on the 1st and 2nd battalions of the Scots dragoon guards but was still not satisfied. Although it was a rousing experience to do it with the girl with no name for the next few months I gave women a wide berth, as I thought that I might have fathered a child and most likely had been infected with VD.

Back on the estate we had chosen a wall outside a church to be our territory. We'd laze about listening to such songs as *Ballroom Blitz* by Sweet and *Rock On* by David Essex on Big Trevor's car radio, along with other classics from that year. Different parts of the estate had been claimed by the crew that lived in or around those particular streets; there was not much left for us so it had to be the church wall. Some people came and went without really being noticed but one clown that no one knew would sit and run everything and everyone down claiming that we were all degenerates – which may or may not have been true but he shouldn't have said it. He was older and bigger than anyone in our crowd and could probably have beaten us in a fight but he was no match for all of us together so one day we kicked his *ballicks* in; he never came back. During these days of respite from the external turmoil the inspiration came for two of my classic poems.

The Inquisitor

I sat alone on our brick wall
It was not difficult at all

Nonsense

Solid is the empty talker
A football in a trance
A cabbage is a wooden stalker
A pair of underpants

There were eight of us that had become really good friends and if we got involved in anything it was all of us or no one. At that time we had our own groupies though most were too young and had faces like busted onions – but at least we had a following. We were a small gang that tried hard to look bad but in fact were not very bad at all – but we did manage to get served in the local pub a few times so we were getting noticed. Along with Billy and Brian the rest were from Brian's school: George; Johnny; Willie; Eddie; and my cousin Jim. He was not a full cousin; his mother and my mother were cousins. We had been friends for over a year before we realised our relationship. I went with him one day to help his granny move some furniture and as we arrived at the block of flats I told him that my aunt also lived there. When he knocked the door I said he must have the wrong place as this was my aunt's flat. He said that I was mistaken as it definitely was his granny's place. We waited at the door.

"Hello Jim," said the old woman, and then looked at me. *"Alan, what are you doing here?"* It turned out my great aunt Sophie was also his granny so suddenly we became cousins and were close friends from then on. George had great natural ability and could have gone far as a footballer but for some unknown reason would hide when any

Irish league scout came for him to try out for their team. He also drank about two pints of milk each day and soon began to put the beef on. Eddie had a real dry sense of humour and was so laid back we'd sometimes not realise he was with us. Willie was as hard as nails, tended to fall in love a lot, was mental about Liverpool FC and went through a phase of staying in listening to his Rory Gallagher and Status Quo LPs. By the time he was 18 he and Eddie had signed up for a three year term with the Royal Marines and I never saw them again. Apparently they both served in the Falklands War.

Johnny was different from the rest. He had a part time job and spent his hard earned savings on a couple of tattoos, one on each arm. On his left arm was a large liver bird and Liverpool FC underneath and on the other arm was King Billy on his white horse. He always wanted to let people think he was connected and liked to roll his sleeves up while sitting in the pub so that he could feel like he was a hard man – hard on the nappies we would say. I was with him when he got the tattoos so the pain he went through as well as the cost was enough to make me sure I didn't get any.

Not long after I got to know Johnny he turned up to a football match with a cast on his arm.

"What happened to you?" I asked.

"I broke it putting my socks on," he replied. Not understanding what I had just heard I decided to ask him how he could have broken his arm putting socks on. Of course it was quite obvious how it had happened. He had been upstairs in his bedroom standing on one leg trying to put a sock on the other foot when he had lost his balance and had fallen out of the window. Luckily for him each council house had a porch above the front door with a concrete roof and that is where he had landed and snapped his arm thus saving him from a full 20 foot nose splat onto the pavement below. If he had landed on his thick head he undoubtedly would have been fine.

Johnny's main problem as he got older was the amount of drink he consumed. His father was an alcoholic and Johnny was well on his way to follow in his unsteady footsteps. There were large arrows chalked onto the footpath that went up to their front door aiding Johnny's dad to get into the house after his usual evening of heavy drinking. By the time he got close to home he'd be on his hands and knees and could follow the arrows that his wife had carefully provided for him.

Anytime we got into an altercation with anyone it was usually because Johnny had caused the problem. One night in a bar he came back from the toilet with an uneasy look on his face and was keen to leave. We decided it was time to move on to another bar so we finished up our drinks. Unfortunately I was the last to leave and got smashed on the head with a bottle by some crazy that had been chinned by Johnny in the toilets because he had stolen his brother's lunch in primary school five years before. I woke up with a barmaid washing the blood and glass from my hair; five stitches later I was as right as rain.

Another incident after the pub which made me feel that there was not much hope for Johnny involved the army and police. I'd made the poor decision of spending the last hour drinking with him and a real *wanker* who was renowned in the estate for being: a real *wanker*. For some reason Johnny liked to hang around with this waster who lied so much he was unsure himself whether his stories were true or not. He would waffle on about how he had shagged women all over the world during his navy days which in fact had consisted of working on the Larne-Cairnryan ferry for a month. On this particular night we walked along a costal path that was adjacent to expensive houses on a street overlooking Belfast Lough that was known locally as *Snob Avenue*. This sea view was not the most majestic in the world, but it was a good spot to watch tankers and other merchant boats sail from the docks as they spewed out oil and waste. Occasionally the odd dead dog with its legs tied together would be washed ashore. What could go wrong on this pleasant tree-lined avenue? As we merrily ambled along Johnny and the other clown climbed onto a Jaguar parked in one of the driveways and started to sing loudly and very badly. Within a couple of minutes a top floor window opened and an extremely irate man leaned out, pointed a shotgun at us and screamed at us to get lost. The sight of the double barrels made us vacate the driveway very rapidly; unfortunately we ran up the street onto the main road and straight into an army checkpoint. We were held for questioning – which was usual when they were bored – and asked for ID. Then a police report came through that three youths had been trying to steal a car in the area we'd just came from so things began to look bleak for us. In those days anyone attempting to steal a car was automatically classed as a terrorist because most bombs planted were in stolen vehicles. When the army received this information it gave them permission to slap us about, throw us into the Landrover and take us back to the police station for interrogation.

Meeting up with my two associates for a drink had been a mistake but walking home with them had been a disaster that would later cause me lots of difficulties when travelling to England

and Scotland. After getting processed they put us in separate rooms. I was positioned in the corner on a chair that faced into the wall, like a dunce at school; this seemed to be standard procedure. A soldier asked me why we had tried to steal the car; I said we had not been trying to steal it and that we had just been messing around. He asked me the question again and when I offered the same answer he delivered a hefty punch into my kidneys and left me groaning and wheezing for breath. With that he left the room and turned the light off, leaving me in the dark. That was it for about an hour until finally a police officer came for me and took me to another, larger room. The other two were already there: Johnny holding his hands together trying to soothe his burnt fingers, and his friend the *wanker* sporting a black eye and rambling on about army brutality. On seeing these two I thought I had got off lightly.

"What did they do to you Johnny?" I asked.

"Nothing," he replied.

"But your fingers?"

He stopped me questioning him any further and said:

"I'm no mug; I saw a Humphrey Bogart film where he put his hands on a stove to burn

off his fingerprints and fool the cops."

He had not been touched by the army or police. As he had been waiting in the room he'd burnt the ends of each finger with a cigarette lighter to prevent them from taking his prints. I shook my head in disbelief as he fidgeted in agony and wondered how I had stooped so low as to have these two in my company. The police already had his fingerprints on record from the last time he'd been in trouble so it was all in vain for the fast thinking Humphrey Bogart type mastermind. This event was put on record as being screened by the army and had me marked by the government as a potential security threat. I would be pulled over and interrogated at various ports of call for the next 10 years.

Easter Monday was a time for civilized people to flock to the beach and get away from the Troubles and the monotonous grind of everyday life, but for one coastal town it was a nightmare. Portrush, a quiet seaside town on the northern shores of Ulster, was a magnet for the youth of inner city Belfast and on one particular day its peacefulness would be devastated. My mates and I joined a troop of boot boys from our estate that had assembled at the local train station for the trip north. We were all pumped up for the day out as we distinguished ourselves from the large skinhead contingent by our immaculate dress code. Most of us wore the same gear: faded denim wrangler jackets, red and black college style jumpers, red parallel trousers and brightly polished Doc Martens – or DMs as they were known locally. Parallels were the in thing at that time and different gangs had their preferred colour. The trousers were available in all sorts of shades: red, canary yellow, electric blue, powder blue, pure white, black, lime green, emerald green and if you were a flash git, Prince of Wales check. None of the Protestant gangs wore green.

The train arrived at the station around nine o'clock in the morning, rocking from side to side and fortunate to still be on the rails. Factions from both York Road and Tiger's Bay had already boarded the train and were in good voice, singing *The Sash* loudly in unison as it pulled in. The chances of getting to Portrush without a rumble would be slim; usually the train arrived with very few windows intact and normally had a police team to greet it. This train was no different; the sound of glass crashing was ever-present on its two hour plus journey which was punctuated by unscheduled stops due to the emergency cord being pulled regularly. Watching out of one of the glassless window frames as the train approached Portrush we could see the police presence awaiting. Just as the locomotive slowed into the platform we heard footsteps above our heads stomping towards the front. Some nutter had climbed onto the roof and had begun running along towards the station. We followed his movements as he jumped from the train top onto the platform roof and then across to a drainpipe which he scurried swiftly down like a drunken gibbon. Sprinting down the main street he punched the first person he saw full on the jaw and knocked him out cold; he was instantly arrested and taken to the cells. His day out in Portrush had lasted as long as it had taken to drop the person that he had chinned.

The first stop in town was at the off-license to stock up on drink to take to the sand dunes before we hit the beach. I bought a half bottle of Haig whisky, something that I had never tasted before but recognised from an ad on the *telly* *"Don't be vague, ask for Haig"*, thinking it would get me in good form for the rest of the day. After we'd downed the various brews it was time to get involved in some action. There had been a few gang fights already with people settling old scores but we did not want to get tied up in all that stuff as we were there for women and a good time. We made the mistake of going into the town centre instead of hitting the beach where I would have probably been better off. I began to sway a bit and felt quite dizzy as we headed towards the rides at the amusement arcade. With nothing consumed other than a bottle of whisky my head began to spin faster than the carousel and bumper cars. A punch-up started between rival gangs and I mistakenly thought that a cousin of mine was in danger of getting a kicking. Like the Tasmanian Devil I ran into the ruck in an attempt to save the day, jumped on an unknown opponent and began to roll around the ground with him. The scuffle lasted a few minutes before being broken up by the police who carted both me and my adversary to an awaiting *paddy wagon* and flung us into the back. Sometime later that evening I awakened to see another kid from my estate looking down and laughing at me and then I realised I was in jail and had missed the last train back to Belfast. My cellmate informed me we were not leaving until we dried out so we would be staying in overnight. It was a long challenging trip back home the next day with a train sparsely occupied by a few freshly-liberated away day convicts. How was I going to explain to my parents that I had been thrown in jail for a drunken brawl and held there until I had sobered up? I felt like a complete waste of space when I finally explained what had occurred. They were not at all happy with my performance but could see that I had been humiliated knowing that all the family knew what a fool I'd been. It could have been worse for me as anyone who had been arrested on Easter Monday had to return for a court hearing the following week. Unexpectedly the charges were dropped and I had a lot of questions to answer from those who attended court as to why I wasn't there.

My dad had recently become a part time police reservist and had managed to get me off thus saving me the trip to Coleraine for a court appearance. A lot of ex-military were joining the RUC to help the overextended security forces. I was shocked when he told me he'd joined up and that I now had to be careful to stay out of trouble as the cops were living in my house. As time went by though I selfishly began to resent him for joining the force even though he had recently bailed me out of trouble and would do so again in the future. For a while our relationship was not great because I began to act like an idiot as I struggled to come to terms with him being a policeman. I know now that my attitude then was completely unreasonable. From then on my temperament began to change as I attempted to portray myself as something that I was not. I wanted to be bad.

My sister had started going out with a boy from her school that was rapidly making a name for himself as being a *hard man* so I thought it would be interesting to see my parents' reaction when they found out. The first time I saw Kathleen and Jim together they waved to me when parting at the top of our street but as she got closer I knew there was a problem. She was giggling and staggering about obviously drunk which was not so good at 15 so I practically slung her over my shoulder and sneaked her into the house up to the bedroom without my parents knowing. It was certainly looking to be the start of an interesting relationship between Jim and my sister. Kathleen was probably getting her own back for the time I had burst into her room when she was asleep and stood on her bed with the ceiling lightshade on my head and asked Scotty to beam me up. Alcohol had also been a factor on that occasion. I knew *Big Jim* through my mates who also went to school with him and he appeared a good lad. In the last year though he had grown taller and stronger than most of us and seemed to be getting involved with people that hung out with the paramilitaries. This made him walk around with an air of being untouchable and he had no problem taking on all comers that were willing to scrap it out with him – he won all the one on one battles. You could almost hear the beat of Gary Glitter's *I'm the Leader of the Gang* thumping out each time he walked by, a very apt tune at that time. People began stopping me on the street asking if my sister was going out with Jim; everyone was talking about it in the area. I had to refer to him as Big Jim to distinguish him from my cousin who now became Wee Jim, mainly because he was wee. Having Big

Jim as a friend could be both good and bad. People who liked him gave me the nod of approval or respect but he had lots of enemies and they had no problem pulling me over in dark alleyways to put the frighteners up me. Times were changing quickly and a lot of 16-year-olds were slipping into the grip of the paramilitaries upon leaving school. These groups used the political unrest for promoting their ideology of being the force that would save us from the Republican threat. My viewpoint of what was occurring during these times was slowly changing and not in a good way.

The carefree summers of lounging by the wall or hanging around the streets were coming to an end. Although Northern Ireland had the highest unemployment rate in the UK nearly all my mates managed to get a job within a year of leaving school. Apart from Billy and I the rest had some type of technical training whereas we were expected to stay on and attempt to gain entrance at a university. Alas for the both of us the benefit of our superior tuition went down the plughole as we started the search for employment before we got our 'O' level results. My chances of finding a job would be slim as there were very few openings available. The dole office had a posting for an assistant to wring out chamois's for a one-armed window cleaner; and another offering a chance to sell surgical wrestling boots to pygmies in the Dungannon area. Not quite what I was looking for.

At that time a special TV message was being broadcast regularly and every time I saw it shivers ran down my spine. It showed a man walking to work. His route each day never changed; he always walked along the same streets. Then one day as he passed a certain landmark at the usual time a gun man jumped out from the shadows and shot him dead. Then an announcer spoke grimly to the audience: "*Never be predictable.*" It was an effort to make people aware that they could be the target of a sectarian attack and that they should be cautious during daily activities. People soon began looking over their shoulder and checked out any sudden movement behind them. Cars slowing down close by made everyone jumpy. It was a frightening time.

People were dying on the streets during these random attacks but life carried on with the help of Belfast gallows humour. As I was ready to join the workforce this piece of film concerned me. I thought about how I could stay safe during my possible future employment and vowed never to be predictable. I would imagine changing my appearance every day by dressing in different attire ranging from Ratty in *Wind and the Willows* to various characters from the *Loony Tunes* cast.

CHAPTER 5

Being Employed

Being at school in the early seventies was quite an adventure. I was old enough to know how bad the Troubles had become but not old enough to let it concern me. Everything changed in the summer of 1973: the comfort of being a schoolboy had come to an end. I had taken my 'O' levels in June and by July I was working as an apprentice butcher at the Co-op. The advantage of having a grammar school education helped me to no end in the butchering business as I used my newfound talents while dismantling various dead beasts and using the bits in many ways. On Monday I'd spend the day with my hand up countless chickens' arseholes scraping out their intestines into a metal bin. On Tuesday and Wednesday I'd make vegetable rolls, sausages and black puddings out of what was left of the inedible animal parts. The rest of the week I was a cleaner, wiping up the blood spatter and guts from wherever it landed as the butchers sliced and dissected their way through assorted cadavers. Before my day was over I had the pleasure to scrub the wooden table block with a wire brush and hot water, which just about made me throw up. While all my mates were working down the shipyard learning trades that could take them to higher levels, I was scrubbing the block.

One good thing about my first job was its location. It was just 10 minutes from my house so I went home for lunch each day although I did smell like an elongated pork chop. As previously mentioned, dogs roamed the open spaces where I lived in packs and unsurprisingly one of these crews hung around the butcher's shop sniffing for a bone. These dogs were smart: I think one of them carried a watch because like clockwork they'd be waiting for me each day at lunch time. I had to run the gauntlet through these slobbering hounds as they pursued the scent of what to them was a large moving, juicy bone. They chased me right up to my house but stopped at the wall and would never come up the path: they had ethics. When my lunch break was over I had to come up with a plan to shake the crazy dogs off. The leader was a tough nut, a big black and white mongrel with part of his left ear missing; his henchmen were mainly made up of the most undisciplined breed in Belfast, the *wee brown dog*. They would loiter around outside talking to each other – some smoking cigarettes;

others doing their nails; all fixated on the smell of the meat and ready to pounce. I thought of leaving via the back but they had a lookout assigned to that exit so my only answer was to dash from the front door and outrun them. This was exhausting but it did entertain anyone who witnessed it. Although it kept me fit my love affair with dead animal parts only lasted three months; I couldn't handle it anymore so it was the dole for me. Of course butchering was only a stop gap until I used my art 'O' level to advance my career. During those lunch breaks away from the butcher's I'd pass the hour writing odd stories and poems and dreaming of being a famous novelist one day. The stories are now lost in the annals of time but my poetry lives on in some rhymes that I called Abstract Limericks.

1. There was a young man called Ken
   Who slipped and swallowed Big Ben
   He said "I don't care"
   And swallowed a chair
   Then jumped on the back of a hen

2. I once knew a man with no throat
   Who lived up a hill with a goat
   His mother went mad
   When he and his dad
   Went down to the pub with no coat

3. There was an ugly wee man
   With a most unusual plan
   He decided to grow
   An extra big toe
   To send to a nun in Milan

4. Alone on a dung beetle farm
   Safe and secure from harm
   When out of a bag
   Came a dwarf with a flag
   And a buffalo under his arm

5. Now Murphy had nothing to do
   So he sawed himself in two
   He unscrewed his head
   Nailed his mouth to the bed
   Then painted his nostrils blue

With no offers from publishing companies I was resigned to the fact that, with the country's unemployment rate at 25%, the chances of acquiring a job or money in the immediate future were slim. I applied for work in the shipyard but it had slowed right down and layoffs were inevitable though most of my friends were there still. The summer was over and the miserable bleak weather was here and I was cheesed off. My school exam test results had arrived so maybe I could use the hard earned four GCE 'O' levels to help me find suitable employment. What advantages did I have over the average unemployed degenerate? I thought that my geography, art, history and ancient history diplomas would surely put me on to the road to financial success but alas they were useless. Five years at grammar school and I was a failed apprentice butcher. Eventually after about six weeks in bed my parents managed to get me a job in the Anderson and McAuley department store as a van boy. I wasn't sure if this was a step up or down from a butcher's mate and with no apprenticeships on offer for van boys I think it was a step down. This job was interesting if nothing else. For the first week I had to work in the store stacking shelves as well as cleaning and sweeping the floors: boring but there were some nice girls there. They would sing and shake their bums to the music being played over the radio and imitate Suzy Quatro's *48 Crash* which would get me all hot and bothered. The older women were dangerous though – unlike the young girls who wouldn't come near me the old bags wouldn't leave me alone. They would constantly grope and molest me, hoping to get me to go bright red with embarrassment, which I usually did. They'd follow me around singing *And I Love You So* by Perry Como. All the fun and games were put on hold one day when a bomb warning was phoned in for the building facing us on Donegal Place. We had to evacuate the store and make our way to the city hall grounds, a safe enough distance away from the bomb location. Almost. As we stood around wondering whether or not it was a hoax an enormous explosion rocked the street as the building blew up and sent hot metal sheets of roofing flying into the air towards the city hall. Luckily the large chunks landed outside the grounds but lots of wee particles showered the uneasy crowd as people body swerved and ducked in an attempt to avoid getting singed. I remember watching one clown dressed in a lovely suit walking over to a rather large piece of smouldering metal that was lying on a patch of the pristine grass lawn. He bent over and picked it up then squealed in agony and flung the object away as it scalded his hand. There's always one.

My first driver at the store was a big fat sweaty *git* who kept burping all day and was constantly pulling his trousers back up over his enormous arse. We met at the store every day to load the van up then we'd head out to deliver all over the city; all I had to do was jump out of the van and take the parcel to its destination. Most of the addresses were in more well-to-do areas so that was fun as I'd never seen the big houses in the Malone area before but every now and again we'd get sent up the Falls

Road. I'd never been up there before except for a trip to the Royal Victoria Hospital but we'd always go via the Donegal Road to be on the safe side. This was one road I did not want to be on – it felt like everyone there knew I was a Protestant and that they were watching me and waiting for the moment to attack. Even Noddy Holder sounded nervous during his rendition of *My Friend Stan* on the van radio. Turf Lodge was the first stop one day; what a dump. It was impossible to find the house we were looking for as all the street names had been painted over with Irish names. We had to ask someone for directions in order to find where to go and each time I'd shit myself waiting for a crowd to drag me out of the van because I was sure that they would know I was a Protestant. Turf Lodge had one road that went right down into the estate then back up out the other side. We had to deliver an electric fire deep into the heart of the grisly place so the plan was to sling the package out at the door and be on our merry way. As I walked up to the house a woman yelled out in distress from behind the partially open front door. I carefully left the fire on the door step but as I was about to leave a large ape type person opened the door and shouted to me:

"*Oi, shite face, where are you goin', what are ya doin' at my door?*" He held the door with one hand and had a woman by the throat in the other. Her face was dripping with blood.

"*Help me, help me!*" she cried.

"*Ah shut up ya slut!*" he screamed at her before banging her face against an adjacent wall. He glared at me and again asked what I was doing at his door.

"*I'm delivering an electric fire from Anderson and McAuley,*" I said nervously, watching the terrified woman sobbing uncontrollably. Then he grunted,

"*well don't leave it there, put it in the living room ya dopey bastard,*" totally ignoring the fact that he was squeezing the life out of somebody. I hesitated. Then three young girls came running down the stairs pushing their way in between the ape creature and his rag doll. Oblivious to what was occurring the kids asked the woman – who seemed to be their mother – when breakfast would be ready. The ape released its grip and let go of her throat; then she got up and hurried into the kitchen. Without a word he looked into my eyes and pointed to where he wanted me to leave the package so I warily eased past him and laid it on the living room floor. My driver and I were up and out of that tip so fast we did not have time to smell what came from my arse as I shit myself.

Another trip up the Falls Road was to be the last for my driver, probably because of me. We had to deliver a pair of stepladders to Father Murphy at the Clonard Monastery, a place that I had heard of but for obvious reasons had never seen. Once again the drive up that road was a nervous one for me; my driver was also a Protestant but he was used to the drive and didn't seem concerned. The monastery was in behind some streets with most of the houses derelict or at least looking that way even though people still lived in them. Any homes that were boarded up had been broken into by the swarms of kids in the area who had made them into one great big playground. They were street kids who looked like they'd never gone home for a wash; they were *piggin'* or *boggin'* as they said in Belfast. Lighting fires and smashing windows was their main pastime. When our van rounded the last street going up to the monastery it was like *Lord of the Flies,* with the herd of youngsters chasing behind flinging bricks and bottles at us. I suppose they didn't get many visitors. I never thought there would be a day when I would be glad to get into a Catholic church.

The monastery was enormous: a glittering gold cathedral standing strong amongst a depraved wasteland. If the priests had given up a few gilded candlesticks, the cash could have gone a long way to feed the surrounding poor. We parked opposite the huge main entrance and I climbed out of the van, stepladders under my arm. My driver barked orders at me to get my finger out and take them to whomever they belonged post-haste. I thrust the doors open and waltzed into the chapel then suddenly felt an eerie numbness all over me. It was the first time that I'd been inside a Catholic church and I was expecting a lightning bolt to strike me down. People were praying in the aisles but didn't seem to take any notice of the skinny Protestant kid walking up to the altar and leaning the steps against the Virgin Mary. It felt like it was the wrong place to put the ladder but I was in no mood to hang around and quickly did an about-turn and headed to the nearest door. The doorway that I left through was not the one I came in but instead led into a large foyer. It seemed to be the residence or living quarters for the monks; it looked like a hotel but no one was there to take my booking. I was busting for a piss and began opening all the closets and cupboards in the corridor but there was no toilet anywhere. In one storeroom I found a large straw laundry basket filled with what looked like the smoky black robes that the *dirty beasts* wore from time to time and as they were already in need of a spruce up I did the deed. Luckily a shite was not required. Feeling a sense of relief I went in search of an escape. I could see the van from a large stained glass window so I walked along the corridor to another doorway. It took me into a loading area that was blocked by a beer truck delivering Harp and Guinness. *This can't be for the monks*, I thought, but I was wrong – one of them was talking to the lorry driver and instructing him to unload a few crates. Drunken monks: they were supposed to be good living. As I *dandered* out towards the van I grabbed a crate for myself and slid it in the side door then stashed it in the warehouse when we got back. The driver was fired soon after that because someone had spotted the van driving off with the nicked crate although he hadn't known that I had taken it. A complaint had been lodged from the monastery so he received his marching orders. He was a bit of a *tea leaf* anyway, pilfering the odd item from various deliveries; I had done the store a favour and he would not be missed.

The job was really a dead end street: there was no opportunity for advancement; my wages were crap; and once again I was feeling pretty useless. Things went from bad to worse when I was involved in a particularly unpleasant incident in the service lift. The lift at work was an old handle-operated type. One day I was sharing it with a large hairy gorilla who worked in the furniture department. Suddenly he unexpectedly stopped it between floors. He asked me if I'd been shagging yet and if I needed any instructions on what to do when trying to slip a hand for the first time. What I didn't know was that this particular orang-utan was a drag queen by night and was not in the least bit interested in women. He leaned over and placed his arms on each side of my shoulders, pinning me to the wall with his big fat hairy ginger belly, which was trying to escape from his trousers. His breath smelt like the gas works and his green teeth rattled as he opened his blotched lips and came in for the kill. Luckily the alarm bell in the lift scared him off just as his hand snaked towards my private parts. That was one department I made sure I would not be alone in again.

November 27th, 1973 was my mother's birthday but it was also a sad day for the family as a very close uncle passed away that evening. It was the first time I encountered grief and it affected me more than I would have thought. Not thinking about the consequences I stayed off work for two days. Upon my return to the department store, I was summoned by the vice president to his big polished wooden office. I'd never been that far up the building before as my interview had been conducted in a dingy smoke-filled room below street level by some middle manager with a wonky eye and a stammer. I knocked on the stained glass door, entered and sat in an awaiting leather chair. I was in territory where not even *van boy* of the year had tread. However, much to my discomfort, there was an audience of people in the room and they were watching everything that was going on. Without looking directly at me, the vice president informed me that the company policy was that only one day off was allowed for grievance. I was still upset and did not have to think too much about telling him to stick his job right up his ring piece: the only time I have ever done what others dream of doing. At 16 it was not a problem. I walked out of the department store around the corner and into the Bank Bar on Castle Street for a pint that was knocked back in a couple of minutes. I decided not to have another as the pictures of Celtic on the wall and IRA posters about the men behind the wire made me realise that the Orange Order did not hold many meetings in there. So I sauntered out down the road and back on the dole again.

Hanging around the estate penniless and bored was a recipe for what we called *badness*. Alcohol was needed for a night out so without money where would I get my supply of some of the finest worldly beverages? The favourite tipples of the street hobo consisted of Bulmer's cider, Mundies full strength South African wine, Scotchmac (*a whams dram?*) and the irresistible Q.C. (*quick corpse?*) sherry/ wine. Not far from the estate was a bottling factory that stocked most of these excellent snifters and was about to shut down because of a strike. The timing was perfect: a building full of liquor but void of people and a housing estate with the available miscreants to take full advantage of the situation. Word spread quickly and a production line was set up: two small nimble people to climb in through an easily-opened window and the rest – about five or six of us – lined up outside moving the bottles along to a top secret location for storage. Within a week the factory was cleaned out as other intruders organized their own capers, which meant we had no chance to go back for more. Police were later called by security guards but it was too late: the damage had been done and no one was ever caught. The perfect crime. A camping trip was soon organised so we pitched some tents near the field where the liquor supply was hidden and got *blootered* for a week. Our parents weren't worried about what we were up to because they were glad we were keeping our noses clean by camping out together.

In January of 1974 I managed to get accepted for one year at a Government Training Centre (GTC) not far from my house. You would be paid a wage in an attempt to learn a trade and hopefully impress visiting companies that might potentially offer a full-time apprenticeship. The idea was to find the strongest skill-set that would suit each individual student by having all of the apprentices work on a variety of different trades for approximately two months apiece. This was a great opportunity provided by the government for out of work teenagers trying to get a leg up. One potential powder keg was that half of the 16-year-olds at the centre were Protestant and the other half were Catholic. During the year I went there, there also happened to be one lone unfortunate Jew. The first question he was asked was if he was a Protestant Jew or a Catholic Jew.

Prior to the start of the course, word went round of who was part of the annual acceptance for the GTC. As the place was situated close to a Catholic area, meeting the others would be safety in numbers on the first day. There were 12 starting from my estate. The majority of them I knew slightly and one of them, Sam, had been a good friend in primary school but we'd lost track of each other since we'd left. The first day we all met at the top of the estate for the short 15 minute walk down the road to the GTC. Just as the main office came into sight we adjusted our walk to the *dander* of *hard men* – this would surely establish us as the main force to be reckoned with inside the building. We signed in, selected the trade we would like to try and pursue after the year was up and then a very ugly nurse with a face like a slapped arse checked us out for fleas and other abnormalities. Six of us, including Sam, had decided we would like to be electricians so that meant a colour bind test was required. It seemed pointless to me; I had to read out large multi-coloured numbers and letters on pages that were shown at random – not a problem at all. We waited in a small room as we took the test one by one. Suddenly Sam burst out of the testing room in tears: he was colour blind which meant he could not train as an electrician. They advised him to try out for a different trade but he was blubbering in despair: all he wanted to be was an electrician. He left the GTC and I never saw him again.

The first month was bedlam: both factions would have mass fights on the street – before work, at lunch time and after work – but as time went by we gradually got to know each other and the religious squabbling died down. Some us even became friends but it was impossible to extend it outside work due to the segregation of the areas. The worst incident happened outside the GTC one evening when a *Stickie* supporter (official IRA) and a *Provo* (provisional IRA) had earlier got into a scrap. The *Provo* whacked the *Stickie* across the head with a metal rake from a lathe; later the *Stickie* retaliated by shooting the *Provo* in the arse cheeks with a zip gun he'd made at work. These two hated each other more than they hated any Protestant in the training centre.

In the midst of all the sectarian mayhem the training staff added a wee bit of the unexpected by playing pranks on the latest batch of apprentices, making them look like right plonkers. I happened to be the first of those plonkers and fell for one of their shenanigans after being sent to the forging area by my instructor. My mission was to pick up three anvil rings to bring back to the electrical section. So off I went feeling good about myself that I should be chosen to carry out such an important task. I went up to the forging instructor and asked for the three anvil rings.

"OK wait there and I'll give you them," the instructor said with a look of annoyance in his eyes. He then proceeded to whack the anvil with a hammer, which made a loud dinging sound; he did this three times then walked away. I stood there picking my nose and hoking the clinkers from my arse and waited for him to get me the anvil rings. After a few minutes he came back out of his office and asked me why I was still standing outside his section. A bit flustered I said:

"I still need the anvil rings."

He replied:

"It was three of them you wanted, right?"

"Aye," I answered.

He went on:

"I've just given them to you, now clear off out of my sight ya dopey bastard."

My jaw dropped. I was unable to respond but I just walked slowly back to my section in a state of total confusion, expecting my instructor to give me shit when I returned, which he did.

"Where are my anvil rings? Go back and do not return until you get them!" he yelled. Even more baffled and slightly worried I turned to go again to the forging section but was halted by my grinning instructor who let me into his cunning secret. He asked me to keep it quiet as someone else would soon be next on his list.

It was a great period. I got selected to play football for the five aside team against other training centres in the Antrim forum and although we lost in the final it was great to be involved considering there were a lot of people trying out for 10 spots on the team. We had special classes about team tactics while the rest of the mugs struggled along filing their metal blocks. During one class I can remember one kid asking the instructor if he got stuck in the corner with the ball could he climb up his own nose. A curious question that resulted in him getting kicked out of the team back to the tools because the instructor did not like people *taking the piss*. Before anyone returned to work after committing a slight misdemeanour they were sent to the punishment bench to cut through a large aluminium block with a hacksaw. This would take over half an hour to get through and then put you behind on any assignment that had been given, thereby forcing you to stay late to catch up. The GTC left me with a lot of great memories and new friends as well as allowing me to finally feel that I had learnt something that could help get a meaningful job. It was the place that I drove a car on my own for the first time – even though I did not have a license – and the place where I met and befriended the Dreaded Catholic, proving that there was not much difference between us. One lasting memory is of my friend from the Shankill, Sammy Bee, climbing onto a work bench during a busy session and standing upright with arms in the air and beginning to sing *The Man Who Sold the World* (the Lulu version) at the top of his voice. The place roared with approval at such a captivating sight and he was saluted with a rapturous applause by the whole factory as he was dragged down and over to the aluminium block by a couple of instructors for his punishment. One poor worker was driven nuts at lunch time by scores of apprentices on their way to the cafeteria. His name was Cahal Moane and his work station was unfortunately located by the main doorway to the lunchroom. He was inundated by the constant chanting of the Wings hit, "*C Moon, C Moon*" from a choir of his peers as they shuffled past.

Having a poor but steady income meant I could finally plan ahead to do something different and maybe get away from this drab war-torn existence. My mate Willie, who was a real Liverpool nut, asked me if I'd like to go to Anfield to see a match and stay for the weekend with friends he knew on Merseyside. I liked Liverpool well enough – although I was not the fanatic he was – and I thought a trip across the water would be brilliant. One of my newfound Catholic workmates, a Liverpool supporter, lent me his scarf and hat; he figured that although he had never been to see a game at least he could say parts of his clothing had. Liverpool was playing Leeds who at that time were the top team in the country. Five of us from the estate had planned the trip together and we met at the docks for the evening sail on the Friday night. A second class ticket on the night before a big game was like a third world boat trip of mass immigrants trying to make it to the shores of a safer haven.

The foghorn blew and we were on our way as we watched Belfast ease out of sight. First class was visible from behind the metal gating: plush cushioned seats and cosy tabled alcoves where people could sit and enjoy a meal and a drink. On the side of the underprivileged various drunks lay sprawled about the floors with all the available wooden benches packed with red-faced bloated fans elbowing each other for a bit of space. Luckily no Leeds fans seemed to have made the journey which reduced the chances of a major ruck. The boat was bunged; it was standing room only. There were seats outside but it was much too cold on deck with the freezing cold surf spraying all around as the boat heaved up and down in the blustery Irish sea. The danger of sliding overboard was made more than a possibility because of all the vomit on the steel flooring. Walking along the passageway was hard enough with the sea swell but the added hazards of skidding out of control on puddles of sick made it lethal: peas and diced carrots everywhere. A couple of nutters, who I knew well, decided to make an attempt at gate crashing first class and with no way through the metal enclosures the only way in was around the outside of the boat. This senseless manoeuvre involved clambering over the railing and scrambling along the edge of the boat then up and over at the first class side. We watched as the vessel rose and fell with the waves: one slip and they would have fallen to their icy certain deaths. No sober man would have dared to have attempted such a feat. Somehow they made it: driven by lashings of cider and lager they'd risked their lives for the lure of the first class delight. Unfortunately for them it lasted no more than 10 minutes – they enjoyed the forbidden luxury all too briefly as it was quite clear the two chancers had broken free of the caged disorder from beyond and they were quickly sent packing back to the dark side.

We docked the next morning sick and hungover and with nothing to eat for breakfast but a couple of cold slices of toast; then we went on to Lime Street for the bus to Seaforth. Belfast had been blown apart during the Troubles: offices destroyed and empty lots cleared of crumbling buildings that had been damaged by relentless bomb blasts. Liverpool was the same as that but without the civil unrest. What a mess. The family that had unwisely agreed to let us stay for the weekend were very hospitable and made us feel welcome. We were introduced to the couple, who were both in their late 20s, and thanked them for putting us up. Sue was a peroxide blonde and although she looked like a bit of a slapper she was in fact a very eloquent woman – if that was at all possible for a Scouse. I'm sure some slappers can be nice ladies also. Wayne was a big bastard and looked like he could have ripped your head right off and probably would have done if you crossed him. Before long we moved down to the pub and then on to the game. The match was a very average one but Liverpool won 1-0 with Steve

Heighway scoring the lone goal. Billy lost his shoe in the Kop so we had to wait until the crowd cleared; unbelievably he found it and saved himself from a long hobble back down the Anfield Road. Missing his true love, he changed his mind about staying and headed down to the docks to get the boat home. That left Willie, Johnny, Fat Bryan and I. So we went back to Seaforth for a fish supper before going to the pub for a few pints: the natural thing to do at the age of 16.

I'd been in a few scuffles before but the evening would end up badly for Willie and me. Fat Bryan was a mouthpiece at the best of times and apparently got involved with a few Everton supporters which resulted in a bit of *argy bargy* at the back of the pub: a few glasses were smashed then the landlord flung us out. Earlier we had met a couple of girls so Willie and I grabbed a carry-out and decided to go to their place to see if we could get a nibble; Johnny and Fat Bryan followed behind. The girls lived in a block of multi-storey flats on a road that was illuminated by the only remaining street lamp that hadn't been smashed in. Before we could get to the front doors we were ambushed by the crowd that had been in the altercation with Fat Bryan earlier. The lights went out in more ways than one as Willie and I got the living shit kicked out of us: we were back to back as they pounded us. I'm not sure why they stopped but the damage was bad enough: we were beaten and bruised covered in blood. Someone must have called for an ambulance because I remember getting treated in the emergency ward but had no idea how we had got there. Willie had three cracked ribs and I had received a broken nose for the first but certainly not the last time.

We arrived back at our lodgings where things began to heat up. Wayne was grunting and groaning and circling the coffee table – revenge was certainly on his mind. Fat Bryan was missing: he'd chickened out and had last been seen running away in no particular direction. Johnny was sitting on the sofa with a gormless look on his face. When Willie confronted him about why he and Fat Bryan had made a rapid disappearance his answer was that he had been kidnapped then beaten and the reason for the lack of cuts or bruises was due to the fact that his skin stretched when kicked. A reasonable answer. Within the next hour about 10 crazy looking thugs arrived in an old beat-up transit van that was tooled-up with axes and hammers; they were intent on doing over our attackers. This was an ongoing feud between two sets of rival gangs. Wayne advised us to leave the area for our own safety and Johnny and I agreed to head for the hills so we spent the rest of the day at St. John's Market waiting for the next boat. Willie on the other hand was staying, as he believed it was his scrap as much as anyone's; he had already begun to sound Scouse and that was after only two days. The outcome resulted in a lot of people getting badly hurt, but not Willie: he was tough bastard, a Royal Marine in the making. He stayed there and became a bit of a legend in the area; he even ended up moving in with the girl he had nearly got off with before the attack. We didn't see him for six months and he came back with a pure Scouse accent.

I'd missed a day at work because of the extra night in Liverpool so rather than go home I went straight to the GTC from the boat, but I was still an hour late. Knowing that everyone at work had already heard of my weekend experience I knew that I would be making a grand entrance. Sporting a busted nose, a large black eye and clothes caked with blood I was greeted with a *"Liverpool! Liverpool!"* chant as I walked through the main doorway. The workmate who had lent me his Liverpool apparel approached me hoping to retrieve his hat and scarf but sadly for him the hat was gone and the scarf was in ribbons. Although it was great to be the centre of attraction for a while I had lost a day's pay at work and it would cost me the price of a new hat and scarf. As well as that my nose had shifted making me look like I was trying to turn left and with my black and white eyeballs an Al Jolson impression was on the cards. Plus I still had to go home to face my mum and dad.

Things were going well at the GTC with most of the apprentices getting on together regardless of the religious divide but as it was Northern Ireland good times were just a warm up for bad things to come. In the summer of 1974 the loyalist paramilitaries brought the country to its knees with a general strike. Going to work was still a possibility but with carloads of masked gunmen driving around threatening those who dared with an appointment at the kangaroo court it was safer to stay at home. It did not make any difference to me – more time in bed – but I had no idea of how bad the situation would become. The paramilitaries began erecting barricades at the four entrances to the estate, mostly stolen cars that would usually end up burnt out. This stopped the police and army from driving into the area but it was soon apparent that it also prevented anybody from leaving, creating a siege type situation – and that was just what they wanted. Groups of youths would hang around street corners getting up to all sorts of mischief. I met with my crowd of pals at the wall where we usually hung around during normal circumstances. Every now and then a car with masked men would pull up and instruct us to gather bottles and stones to prepare to attack the security forces. All the prepared missiles were taken to certain locations as people waited for the organised riot to occur. The idea was to harass the army and police and tie them up while the boys in hoods did a few bank jobs. Bands of teenagers roamed the estate looking forward to flinging some rocks and bottles but to law-abiding adults it was very stressful, particularly for people worrying about the whereabouts of their sons or daughters. As the power plants closed down then obviously we were to be without heat and electricity. Most families were prepared with candles to light up the rooms and coal-burning fires to keep the chill out on those July nights; it was a tough period but we managed to survive the anarchy of vehicles burning, youths rioting and sirens wailing each night.

Organised rioting was common and one time we had hand-to-hand combat with a rival gang near the GTC centre, which mainly consisted of people punching and kicking each other without weapons. The army came in to clear up the mess and scooped up about 20 youths – including myself – off the street and into their armoured trucks to take us to a hall for interrogation. On this occasion we were ordered to lie flat on our stomachs, hands behind our heads. They banged on the floor with their batons for about 10 minutes then turned off the lights and warned us not to move. After lying still in the same position for about an hour we were released to the streets with no charges. It had all been mind games. My parents never thought that I had been involved in the mass scrap mainly because they knew the crowd I hung around with were smarter than the average delinquents. Almost. Although it was unusual for us to join in the fighting this had been a big one involving most of the estate; normally we were not too militant and knew when to step down. One of my mates had got a brick between the eyeballs when he had been caught in crossfire during a riot with the army. It had been a bad gash and getting treatment had been difficult as the hospitals were barely functioning. I think this had put us off getting totally involved although word soon spread if you were not participating in the cause and you risked the wrath of the paramilitaries. Gunfire was in the air most nights: usually a bit of target practice at various objects but a lot of kneecapping took place for unknown reasons. One time, a few of us were walking up from the bottom of the estate when we heard the distinctive *crack! crack!* of a pistol being discharged. As we got closer to the incident a woman came running towards us covered in blood; she was screaming for help. She stopped as we approached; there did not seem to be any wounds on her body but she was pointing frantically to a nearby alleyway. Someone was groaning in agony so we proceeded with caution before encountering two bodies about 20 yards apart with blood pouring from their legs. Two brothers who we knew had been kneecapped; they were bad little bastards always up to no good and although they had not deserved such a severe punishment they had known the risks. Kneecapping was a macabre art form of those times: a pillow over the knee and one shot from behind on the inside of the leg and the kneecap was blown off. Doctors at the Royal Victoria Hospital were so used this type of surgery they became worldwide experts in kneecap replacements. Other times when ammunition was short the torture was carried out using a drill; *"Black and Decker, Black and Decker"* was the threatening call of the night.

In July most of my mates went to Largs in Scotland but Billy and I, along with two school friends Paul and Thomas, went back to the Isle of Man for the third year in a row, staying in Douglas. Belfast was starved of musical entertainment during the Troubles but we were able to see the big name bands of that time such as Slade, Mott the Hoople and the Doobie Brothers inside the packed Villa Marina. At the end of the promenade rusted metal steel frames stood as a grim reminder of the disaster that had occurred when the magnificent Summerland complex had burnt down the previous year. The resort had opened in 1971 and had been a climate-controlled building that had been constructed to blend into part of the surrounding hillside. It had been five floors high, all indoor, and the top deck had mainly been for sunbathing below the clear plastic dome. The middle floors had been full of restaurants and bars and there had been a stage show matinee during the day. At night discos and dancing had taken place on the bottom level where a large swimming pool had been lit up along with the existing waterfall which had been its source. We had bought a weekly pass and had spent the week enjoying the many activities on offer, such as laughing at the talent shows which had been decided by how loud the audience had cheered. Tragically Summerland had burnt down the week after we left; 50 people had died, most of them in agony as the plastic dome had melted and fallen onto the sunbathers below. Because the roof materials had been plastic a lot of the victims had been asphyxiated by the billowing toxic smoke. This catastrophe had been the result of some kids playing with matches in a coatroom in the basement. Ten days earlier and we would almost certainly have been in it.

Billy and I met two girls from Stockport – Barbara and Michelle – who were keen to hear about the events of Summerland and we ended up seeing them each day until the week was done. Barbara and Billy lost touch with each other but I travelled to Stockport regularly over the next three years to see Michelle. As she had two brothers and four sisters it was always packed in her house. On one occasion she asked if we could go some place where we could be alone so I took her to a Stockport County game against Workington Town at Edgely Park. The game was quite exciting considering it was in league division four and although Stockport had most of the chances Workington won comfortably in the end 3-1 and sent the sparse crowd of Stockport supporters home licking their wounds. Stockport had been relegated from division three the previous season and it was obvious that the team would struggle again even though division four was a weaker one.

My trips to England became more difficult on my meagre income and Michelle did not fancy a visit to Belfast so I decided not to go back for a while, especially after an uncomfortable incident with her hairy-arsed older brother. He was 24, an ex-soldier and over six foot, and he still lived at home with his parents and three sisters. Michelle and the others had gone to bed but he had convinced me to stay up and have a late night drink with him so that we could get to know each other better. I thought it would make a change from listening to George McCrae telling me to *Rock Your Baby*: a song that the girls played constantly. As we got drunker he determined that he should give me a blowjob which sent me into a panic, as I was shocked that he'd never even asked for my permission. When he went to the kitchen for another bottle of Bacardi I was out of the living room and up the stairs like Jesse Owens at the Berlin Olympics. I locked the bedroom door behind me and pulled the wardrobe over the entrance. I did see Michelle again but by then it was safe enough for me as big brother had gone off to work down south somewhere.

The GTC had introduced me to new friends from different parts of Belfast, particularly from Sandy Row, a tough and staunch Loyalist area. I began to spend more time at the houses and pubs around these streets and also got to know some real crazy people. Three of my pals were Colin and Mike from Sandy Row and Sammy from the Shankill; all of us worked together at the GTC. One summer's evening, on one of my first visits to Sandy Row, I was standing outside a bar on the Donegal Road having a quiet pint with Colin and Mike. This was new to me as I would never have contemplated drinking outside my own comfort zone in such a tough neighbourhood that was largely controlled by the UDA. I felt good and it seemed nice and relaxed, not like the heavy hype that went along with the area. It was getting dark and the street lights began to flicker to life. We were babbling on about this and that when out of a side street a beat up old Ford Cortina screeched to a halt and out jumped a masked man with a shotgun. He shouted out,

"*Up the Donkey Dick Freedom Fighters, DDFF forever!*" then pointed his gun upwards and with both barrels blasted the street light to pieces; then he jumped into the car then disappeared as quickly as he had arrived. Now covered in glass we slowly crawled out of the pub doorway that the three of us had impulsively dived into. I looked at Colin and Mike, astonished by what had just happened

"*Welcome to Sandy Row,*" Colin said with a grin that looked both concerned and nonchalant and the same time.

"*Who the hell are the Donkey Dick Freedom Fighters?*" I asked.

"*They're a load of drunken eejits that drive around shooting up things that aren't human, mainly street lights and phone boxes. No religious connections, they're just mental.*" *OK*, I thought. *That's all right then, nothing to worry about.* I got to know a few of Colin's friends: a real mixed bag of likely lads, some a good laugh and some a couple of shillings short of a pound. The crazies were mostly Mike's mates. Colin was a good lad but Mike had a real short fuse. One of his ear lobes was sliced due to a time he had had an earring torn from the side of his head during a fight; he had ended up glassing his attacker in return. When I went up to Sandy Row I was meeting with Colin; Mike was not always there and that was a good thing. Mike was to end up in morgue a few years later after he was found stabbed in an alleyway near the town centre. It was sad but he slowly spiralled out of control and ended up with a death wish that came true.

One of Colin's mates that I really liked was Big Stevie. He was a couple of years older than me and a wannabe UDA man; I never knew if he was in it then or if he eventually joined up. He was unique and eccentric along with a *dander* of all *danders* as he walked down the street with arms hanging down and out to the side, shoulders forward and the head nodding to one side every fifth step or so, so that he gave off the appearance of a large flightless bird. He was not a stupid man but he was no brain surgeon. His image was really important to him: he was always well-dressed but not too fancy, more uniformed with a blazer or sports jacket like an old retired general. Most people thought he was a hard man with connections and although he did know some disagreeable characters Stevie was really not a bad lad at all. Still anyone that crossed him usually ended up with a slap as he was a big lad that could handle himself.

He had just bought an old maroon Sunbeam Alpine for about 50 quid and no doubt thought that having a car would boost his image, or so he believed. One night a crowd of us were hanging around the back streets bored stiff with nothing to do when the entertainment turned up in the form of Big Stevie and his 1966 Sunbeam.

"What ya think?" he enquired. *"Want to go for a spin downtown?"*

Someone shouted:

"Clear aff Stevie, I wouldn't be seen dead in that banger; what happened to the convertible you were going to get?"

Stevie had always said his first car would be a convertible and was really pissed off that we were not interested or impressed with his new wheels. He pumped the accelerator in a show of defiance then eventually after a few backfiring farts trundled out of sight. We had upset him and really should have given the heap a nod of approval as he did strange things when disturbed. The next day we were back in the same place doing the same thing: scratching our arseholes and talking shite. Once again Big Stevie drove up to where we were but this time he got a big reaction from us. We took one look at the newly modified boneshaker and shook our heads in disbelief: it was now a convertible. He had cut the roof off. Along the door frames and back window the pointed jaggy metal parts were covered in foam rubber which was held in place by loads of sticky tape. The car rattled and banged as he sat idling in his customised work of art with a grin like a Cheshire cat; he finally had a convertible. After an initial silence we all broke into fits of uncontrolled laughter and once again Stevie drove off in disgust like a wounded animal. Later that night he took the car behind some derelict houses and set it on fire, much to the entertainment of the kids in the surrounding streets. They had quite a party as they danced and sang for ages around the flaming custom-built sports car.

When I was not hanging around Sandy Row Colin and I would meet up with Sammy on the Shankill Road. Colin was seeing a girl from there and one night he had arranged to meet her in the Loyalist Club where she worked as a barmaid. This club was well-known for being frequented by the paramilitaries; I knew of the place but didn't know of anyone from my area who drank in this covert establishment. I was wary of entering the club alone so I asked my mates Jim and Johnny to come with me. Johnny was really up for it as it would increase his stature on the street when word got around that he been in the Loyalist Club. Colin decided to meet us in a bar close by before we went into the club which was better for us as guests had to be signed in by a member. We were a bit nervy about entering due to the interrogation the security guards put us through before we got the all clear. Sammy lived a couple of streets away and had been in with his cousin a few times before. Although Colin was not technically a member of the club his girlfriend's dad was the bar manager and had enough clout to get us past the very intimidating doormen. My first impressions of the place were favourable. I'd expected a dark, seedy drinking den full of unshaven gangsters but the main room had a spacious dance floor and stage at one end and a set of double doors at the other end that led into a large brightly lit bar. It was early evening with a sparse crowd scattered from table to table. There were a few unexpectedly smart-looking girls with well-dressed partners awaiting the evening's main act, which was a local country and western band. *This is all right,* I thought as we looked for a decent table.

"*Let's go to the back bar to see Jean,*" said Colin.

"*We might get a cheap drink.*" That sounded like a good move as the only thing better than a cheap drink was free drink. But it was a bad move; we should have stayed in the main hall because this was the bar the wise guys hung out in and they were a scary bunch of bastards. We swigged back a whiskey each and decided to get back to the other room, hopefully without being noticed. But before we could make it to the door for a quick escape a big geezer in a black leather jacket, obviously quite inebriated, approached us and gestured at Sammy to come to him. Sammy walked nervously forward to the imposing figure, glancing over his shoulder at us and hoping that we had his back. The man held up one hand to stop him and with the other opened his jacket up to reveal a pistol wedged into his belt. We all froze. This was not turning out to be a good first visit. There was an endless pause before the silence was broken.

"You tell your cousin if he doesn't come in here soon to sort out the situation he's going to need new knees."

He burped, farted, then turned and staggered out of the club. Sammy was motionless; the rest of us slinked away from the lingering bad stench in the air that was possibly coming from our petrified friend who may have just shit himself. Even though this incident was a bit threatening the intoxicated gunman never returned and the rest of the evening went trouble free. Welcome to the Loyalist Club.

In the spring of 1974, the day that I had been awaiting for what seemed like forever finally arrived: I was old enough to drive. My plan was to take my test, buy a car and be an irresistible cool dude, pulling loads of girls to join me on trips in my new wheels. Not having any money didn't seem to enter into the equation. A couple of months after turning 17 I applied to take the driving test after my dad had taken me out a few times and although he recommended that I get more experience, I knew better. The inspection office was on Duncairn Gardens and although the name paints a pretty picture it was a road that ran from north to south splitting two of the roughest and most dangerous areas in the city. To the left side was the Catholic New Lodge with its giant multi-storey flats and to the right was the Protestant Tiger's Bay, which meant that a continuous sectarian conflict was a way of life on these streets. It was a sunny Tuesday afternoon and I was confident that I'd do well. My dad took me to the office and left me outside in the Triumph Toledo that I had taken lessons in so I felt good as I waited for the examiner. I was greeted by an anxious spotty little man who seemed to be in a rush.

"OK, head up the Gardens until I tell you to stop," he said.

Great, he's just letting me go for it, I thought. *This will be no problem.* So off we went. About 10 minutes into the test he abruptly pointed to shop and wheezed:

"Pull over here."

Surprised at the sudden demand I almost hit the curb but managed to straighten up in time. He jumped out and hurried into the shop, eventually emerging with a pack of cigarettes, his hands shaking as he lit one up and shoved it into his sweaty mouth. *What's all that about?* I thought. *I'm supposed to be taking a test, not doing his messages for him.*

"Keep going up the road," he snarled. I began to feel uncomfortable having this miserable twitchy toad man beside me. As we neared the top of the road I had to pull the steering wheel sharply to my left to avoid being demolished by a large military Saracen armoured truck that came ploughing towards me at high speed. I crashed up onto the pavement and spun around facing down the road. The truck swerved to a halt and blocked the road; then soldiers jumped from the back and crouched by the vehicle.

"They're up there!" one soldier shouted, pointing to a block of flats to his right. Then *crack! crack! crack!* a gun battle broke out between the army and the IRA.

"Let's get out of here!" yelped my terrified instructor. Still shaken I restarted the car. Somehow I managed to compose myself and drove away from the ensuing crossfire and back towards the office of the driving school. I have no recollection of that

short drive. Upon arrival my bloated little examiner shuffled some papers into my hand and as he hurriedly exited the car announced that I had failed the test. Uncertain as to what had just occurred I sat completely still, waiting for my dad to come out. When I explained the situation he went back into the office ranting and raving at the receptionist and demanded to see my examiner – but he had done a runner out the back door. They agreed to let me take my next test free of charge. The driving school was relocated a few months later to a safer location at the south of the city after an instructor was hit by a stray bullet. No driving license and no car kept me stuck to the same old routine: loitering about the estate. I was able to walk to the GTC but my year's training was almost complete and being able to drive would have given me an edge when trying to find permanent employment. A few apprentices had been flung out of the GTC because their work hadn't been up to standard so I had to try and get better marks to impress the companies that were seeking the best trainees. With four electrical groups seeking work and eight trainees in each section it would be difficult to find placements for all of us, particularly my group as our marks were the lowest. As each week went by nothing was coming my way and it looked like I'd be back on the Dole in less than a month's time. Finally a break came, not from an electrical company but from an outfit that installed and maintained lifts. They were looking for four apprentices: three to work from their Belfast office and one to work at their new manufacturing plant in Bangor. We were assured that there was a lot of electrical work involved so our training would be an asset. Billy from Sandy Row, Paul from Glengormely and I were chosen to join the maintenance branch in Belfast and because his marks were not as good Sammy was offered the Bangor job. None of us had any idea about how a lift worked but it was a job and no one complained. The new employees would be used as slave labour – similar to chimney sweep kids – cleaning everything that went up, down or stood still. Some of my favourite jobs were in the abattoir, the gut and tripe lift and the intestine conveyor. Lovely.

We left the GTC and began our apprenticeship, working on lifts with no concept of what went on in the trade or how any of us would cope, though for the first couple of months no technical training was needed to clean out escalators and lift shafts. We finished each night completely *boggin*, covered from head to toe in oil, grease and dirt. No overalls were provided so our clothes took a lot of abuse and sometimes we were refused entry onto the buses when going home.

The company was made up of about 50% of each religion – not including Jewish or Muslim – and employees came from all parts of the city. After six months I managed to get my cousin Jim started as the firm won a large contract with an abattoir that was modernizing 12 lifts and therefore needed a couple more apprentices. He went straight on construction working with a fellow who had been previously employed by the company but had had a break in Long Kesh after a robbing a bank. The rumour going round was that he was a full blown mental case and nobody wanted to work with him, so that's why Jim was given the job. It turned out well for him though as it wasn't all true: he was only half mental.

For me it was down to the slaughterhouse with my engineer from East Belfast, who was affectionately known to most people as Smelly Clark. I had not met him before as he had been working in Dublin with another apprentice but when I finally had the pleasure of my first encounter with him all the lines from my colleagues began to make sense. If we passed a raggedy old coat lying on the roadside they would point and simply say, "Jimmy Clark's coat"; or an old pair of shoes it would be, "Jimmy Clark's shoes"; or any other item of soiled clothing: it was always Jimmy Clark's. He was probably in his 40's – though he looked like he was

50-odd – and he stunk like a cow's arse. The old jacket that he always wore had probably been flung out by a tramp; his shirt collar would have been a good place to grow spuds; and the soles of his shoes flapped in the wind. His matted greying hair was a bird's nest full of the remnants of the week's previous jobs. He was a mess.

I was looking forward to finally doing some electrical work; the first job was to rewire the hall push buttons on one of the lifts. I will never forget the feeling of walking through the huge steel doors for the first time: the sordid ambience of the abattoir hit me almost immediately. The smell of death was all around; it was a cold, damp and bloody place. As I walked through the main factory to the job we were about to work on my eyes glistened at the horrendous spectacle in front of me. It was a mass production line. At one end a crazy-looking man with a long electrical probe zapped the cows to make them walk towards their ultimate demise. Each cow would reach an open metal enclosure where there was barely enough room for them to stand. Another crazed man waiting above the metal pen would then prepare a *Star Wars*-like hydraulic bolt gun that was on a flexible bracket at the front of the enclosure. As the animal stood helpless and oblivious to its fate the gun was placed on its head and was then fired. The cow stumbled as the bolt plunged into its brain. Next, one panel of the enclosure opened and allowed the heavily sedated cow to fall over onto its side; then a winch was lowered and a sling was looped around its back leg. Within seconds the cow was raised into the air, dangling face down as it was driven along a track. Blood-soaked men holding various tools and dressed like something from The Texas Chainsaw Massacre stood at different locations below the track and waited for the stunned beast to arrive at their stations. The first stop was at a machine with a claw grip that was attached to the tail; in one movement the clasp was lifted which in turn tore the hide completely off the cow. The skin was then deposited along with previous hides into a container which was carted away when it was full. Within minutes at three different stops the animal had had its legs and head cut off and was completely gutted and ready to be carved into sections for the butcher's shop. Upon leaving the main factory I witnessed the final macabre scene: a metal wheelie bin stacked with eyeless, bloodied skulls. It resembled the aftermath of a nuclear attack.

We made our way from the execution chamber down a spiral staircase into a damp dimly lit room to the lift that needed to be rewired. I just wanted to go home as I was shivering and feeling sick to my stomach after watching the barbaric act of the animals being sliced up. The walls of the room were covered in a sticky glue-like substance that smelt extremely bad. On one side of the room there were two rectangular metal bins positioned below chutes in the ceiling; the lift was at the opposite end. Smelly Clark began dismantling the push buttons and occasionally asking me to pass him whatever tool he required. As I shuffled around trying to keep warm a swooshing sound became noticeable; this was followed by a banging splatting noise and suddenly Jimmy and I were covered in shite. I took cover inside the lift car as my raggedy superior carried on working without batting an eyelid. Minutes later it happened again but this time I was sheltered inside the lift as I watched the flying manure settling onto Jimmy's shoulders and into his hair. Still he continued working.

"Where's this stuff coming from Jimmy?" I asked.

"After they cut out the cow's insides and shite bags the stuff slides along stainless steel drains and then falls into those chutes down to the bins," he casually replied.

"This is a gut and tripe lift we are working on," he continued.

"Oh aye, now you tell me," I said, resigned to the fact that I'd be back the next day to continue this mental torture. In fact I was there for over a month: sweeping, cleaning and scraping bits of animal

innards off various locations then painting the lifts to make them look like new. Nausea and anxiety greeted me during my first week at the abattoir but as time went by I got used to the killing and blood spatter and found it easier to eat meat again.

My next job was at the shipyard on a super tanker helping to install two lifts that were to travel 14 floors through the hull up to the bridge. The giant yellow cranes Samson and Goliath were always busy trundling along their tracks carrying massive metal parts to various locations and I was lucky enough to take a ride up one of Goliath's legs for a fantastic view of the city. It was amazing to watch all the different trades involved putting together these enormous ships section by section and then ultimately making the things float. I was there for three weeks and enjoyed the challenges of installing the lifts but a tragic event occurred that shook everyone who worked there. A young welder was crushed to death when he was hit by one of the giant cranes as it moved along the dockside track. Everyone was deeply shocked by the incident and the yard lost the easy-going atmosphere that it had had before. He had only been 21.

Soon it was time for me to move from construction to work with a maintenance engineer. The term engineer was used very loosely as the fellow I was to assist was only 19 and had not yet finished his apprenticeship. But he had a moustache and being two years older than me he seemed ancient. Tony was from the New Lodge which meant he was a Catholic so I was wary of how our partnership might evolve. He had long wiry hair, slightly hunched shoulders and walked with a swagger: typical of someone from the New Lodge. Most of his jobs were in the city centre, which meant he did not have a van as it was impossible to park it anywhere, so we either walked or got the bus. On our first day together we went to a job on College Street; he *dandered* on ahead and I followed with his canvas tool bag. We climbed a ladder up to the machine room where I saw a controller of a passenger lift for the first time. It looked really complicated with contactors and relays snapping in and out as the lift travelled up or down. When he asked me to pass him his tool bag I thought that at last I was going to learn something technical instead of using a brush or a rag to clean something. He picked up his bag and carefully placed it in front of a radiator under the window where he lay down and then, using the sack as a pillow, went to sleep. For a moment I stood frozen trying to piece together in my mind what had just happened. After a few minutes I looked around the room and found a nice spot where I too laid down for a wee snooze. About an hour later I was awakened by the sound of Tony's broad accent.

"Wake up ya lazy bastard, if you wanted to sleep ya shud have stayed at home in yer bed." I jumped to my feet in a panic trying to apologize to him and he laughed.

"Only messin' ya around, it was a decent sleep OK." This was the start of a great friendship and we did sleep together again on another day when we dozed off on the roof of the Murray Tobacco factory only to be awakened by the five o'clock horn. On that occasion he was annoyed because we were supposed to finish at 4:30 p.m. so he told me to book half an hour overtime. Tony had a great sense of humour and had me laughing most days. I remember his description of an incident that had occurred at a party that his wife had dragged him to. He explained to me with a cheeky grin:

"I was lookin' around at all these arse holes when I let rip with one of the smelliest farts I've ever done then all of a sudden, such a scatterin' match, people were runnin' for the doors and windies to escape the stench. I was done for though as my wife knew it was me as I was the only one left in the room."

His account of the scene had me roaring as he moved his body about as he did the actions and painted the picture perfectly.

Each Monday we received an allowance from the office for any bus fares required. Tony would rather walk to the jobs and keep the money for lunch, which we usually had in the pub. One job that we had was up the Falls Road and Tony asked if I was all right to take the stroll as it was within my rights to refuse. I remembered that the last time I had gone up that road my bum had been twitching a lot – and now there was even more IRA presence than before. The idea of me walking up there was terrifying but as I was a mug full of bravado I said that it would be no problem to accompany him on the march of fear. It had been safer going up the road on my last visit as I had been in a van, but even then it had felt like everyone had been watching me, staring suspiciously at the terrified kid that looked like a Protestant. This time as we took that long, long trek I was convinced that I was done for because they'd all hear my knees rattling together in fear. Why had I said yes to this madness? Eventually we somehow reached our destination alive although I was sure they'd get me on the way back down. We turned off the main road into some back streets and my heart was pumping so fast my jacket was moving in and out. I just wanted to get to where the job was and get off the streets. Everything looked eerily familiar to me and as we rounded the last bend, there it stood, in all its glory: once again I was at the Clonard Monastery. For a second time I was to enter the vast, gleaming cathedral. On this occasion though I was not a mere van boy but a budding lift engineer so I gathered up my courage and prepared to once again wander through the corridors of the gloomy smoke-filled residence that stank of mothballs and paedophiles. At the main entrance to the priests' apartments stood the old lift with beautiful brass fittings and a wrought iron shaft that travelled 4 floors to the penthouse suites. Perhaps the chief diddlers of children were housed on the top floor. The priests were creepy creatures, wandering around the monastery like vampires as if waiting to lure their prey to their nests; I felt uneasy watching them shuffle around. The machine room for the lift was located in a glass dome on the roof that had views right across the city. To my left was the Falls Road leading up to the Royal Victoria Hospital and to my right was the Shankill Road running up to Glencairn. There was to be no sleeping in this machine room.

Close by was an old factory that had been converted into an army barracks and on the roof was a gun post that surveyed the streets for potential trouble. I could clearly see the soldiers having a smoke and resting on their rifles inside a sandbagged lookout post. Suddenly they began to scramble around, pulling on their helmets and swinging their rifles to point towards the Falls Road. Both Tony and I instinctively shifted to look left where we saw a sniper on the rooftop of the Divis Tower flats; within seconds we saw a flash coming from his rifle then heard the *crack!* of gunfire. Turning quickly back in the other direction we saw the same from the army and heard what seemed like 20 to 30 *crack! crack! cracks* as they engaged each other. We both froze as glass shattered above our heads: the dome had just taken a hit and we were showered with small sharp particles that littered the machine room floor. We dived in unison to the floor and covered our heads with our hands. The gun battle lasted for about five minutes but felt like an eternity as we lay on the ground unable to move until it had ended. Once the commotion had subsided Tony and I evacuated the building within seconds, not stopping until we were back on the main road and waiting for the next bus back into the city centre. By this time all sorts of creatures had crawled from their holes to see who was getting shot at, some of them dancing and singing songs in support of the IRA. That was it: the only way I was ever going back into that area was in a tank as I never wanted to be in that monastery or on the Falls Road again. Tony and I became really good friends at work but that's where it ended; we could never go into each other's areas which in itself was a great shame.

CHAPTER 6

Behind the Wheel

On December 6th, 1974 I successfully completed my driving test on the second attempt, this time in the safer location of the Boucher Road on an industrial estate in South Belfast. This was a much more relaxed test with no one shooting at me and an advantage of having an instructor who was the uncle of one of my workmates at the GTC. Everything went smoothly and I was at last licensed to cruise the country – well in my mind at least. Once I got back home I sprinted down to Willie's house to tell him of my success; he was in listening to *Dog of Two Head* by Status Quo with the volume pumped. He looked over with two thumbs raised.

Most of my crowd met that evening at the pub to celebrate and discuss the upcoming adventures on the open highway although there was the slight snag of not having a car. I was already on my dad's insurance so the next move would be to try and borrow his newish Triumph Toledo. He had no problem with it and allowed me to drive around the estate at first to get used to being on the roads by myself. Two girls that sort of fancied me called round after hearing the news that I'd passed my test and asked if we could go for a spin. It was a start even though at 15 they were two years younger than me – but one had to start somewhere. Off we went cruising the estate playing some tunes. Unfortunately the selection of tapes my dad had for the old eight track cassette was not the kind of music that would impress the women so it would have to be Neil Diamond over Jim Reeves. With *I Am I Said* blasting out we drove to the places where there would be an audience; I was secretly hoping to catch the eyes of future ladies who I could take with me on the next cruise. We pulled over into a layby with a lovely view of the harbour docks: a perfect place for a shag, but as my passengers were both under 16 it was out of the question unless I wanted to become the youngest paedo in the estate.

Because of the dangerous situation involving car bombs insurance was extremely expensive, especially for young drivers. At that time no car could be left unattended in certain areas of the city centre and each car had to have a means to demobilise it in the event that it was stolen. Failure to do so would result in a hefty fine, sometimes more than the vehicle was worth as there were a lot old scrappers on the road.

One weekend my dad was in London visiting his brother so I put pressure on my mum to let me take the car to a friend's house in South Belfast. As we lived in North Belfast it would be the farthest trip I had taken to date so with some resignation she gave me the keys. Wee Jim called round and off we went to Dunmurray to see my mate. We ended up in the pub for a drink but being extra cautious I held myself back to a half of lager while the other two sunk a few pints each. At 11 o'clock the pub closed and we were on our way back across the city. In Northern Ireland the law was to have a red R plate displayed on the front and back of the car as there was a restriction to drive for the first year below 45 MPH and I made sure of staying at that speed especially after a beer. A recent four lane addition of the motorway had been completed and seemed to be the most convenient route to take home. New adjoining lanes to the extension were slightly curved with a bit of a ramp, and as I had never seen them before they took me off guard. I recall taking the bend at a reasonable speed in the middle lane then accelerating when straightening up. On my outside a car travelling recklessly fast whizzed past, causing me to lose concentration then control. It felt like everything was in slow motion as my dad's new car began to spin around and around as if in a bizarre waltz. We smashed into the centre median, which caused our bodies to lurch forward and strike the dashboard; then the car rebounded and began careering out of control. In a wild panic I began to frantically turn the steering wheel from left to right. This made the situation worse, and we skidded across all four lanes, somehow miraculously avoiding the traffic that was attempting to avoid us. There was no way of stopping the runaway vehicle as we primed ourselves for another impact, this time into the inside barrier. Thinking about it now, most of the accident is as clear as a bell to me apart from when we actually crunched to a halt, although I do remember the sound of glass shattering and metal twisting. The following moments were a complete blank; the next thing I can recall is standing on the hard shoulder pulling hopelessly on the bumper of the crumpled smouldering car front and shouting:

"Jim, Jim, the car's wrecked! Help me, my da will kill me!"

My eyes shifted to the passenger seat and I realised he was unconscious; his head was through the side window covered in blood and glass. I tried to drag him out of the car but he was a dead weight and in my struggle to free him a severe pain shot through my chest. The steering wheel had whacked into me with a lot of force on impact so it was possible some ribs were busted. Jim started groaning; I began to flap a bit as I began to worry that the car would soon burst into a ball of flames. He came round enough to let me help him get far enough away from the potential fire hazard for us to feel safe. We watched and waited for the explosion but it did not happen. No one seemed to be interested in our plight as car after car sped past the scene. Every now and then we'd hear the odd *"wankers!"* shout or receive a two fingered salute from some real helpful people. With no phone available we were on our own. After about ten minutes we felt the risk of a blast was slim so I got back into the car and tried the ignition: it started the first time. The thing was a write-off but I still managed to turn it over; with no other way to get home our only option was to try and drive. Reverse gear didn't work so with both of us yelping in pain I pushed it back off the barrier and managed to start moving the car forward. Usually cops were everywhere arresting people if they farted too loudly but when we needed help they were missing in action. Cars flew by us on the motorway, blasting their horns as we struggled along very slowly using only first and second gear. After about an hour we had rumbled the two miles up the road from the accident and had finally arrived at my house. Since passing my test, every time I finished driving around the estate I'd come into the house claiming that I had smashed the car up to see my mum's reaction but she soon learned to ignore me after a while. On this occasion it was the boy who cried wolf as I dragged myself whinging into the living room where my mum was sitting talking to my Aunt Lily while my sister and Big Jim watched TV. I groaned softly:

"The car's smashed up,"

"Aye, away on with ye, heard it all before," replied my mum without even turning round. I looked at Big Jim.

"Honestly, the car's wrecked; give me a hand to get it to the garage."

He knew that this time it was the truth and calmly followed me to the front door where Wee Jim was standing in the street, still in shock. Between the three of us we managed to get the car round to the back of our street to the garage we rented along with the house. My uncle came over to see what damage had been done, then called my dad in London to tell him that his car was a write-off which caused him to panic but he was relieved to find I was unharmed. It was the last time that my dad let me drive any of his future cars for a while and he terminated any insurance policy with my name on it.

All my plans of cruising around visiting different towns were put on hold as I went from being free as a bird back to being a prisoner confined to public transport. The accident had put me off driving; I now had the same uncertain feeling about being behind the wheel as I did on the day that I had failed my first test. There was not much to do locally so the city centre became more appealing and I began to spend time after work having a drink in Sandy Row or the Loyalist Club. Every Thursday following our last job we'd end up back at the office and occasionally I'd walk to the bus stop with a girl that worked in the building opposite. Her name was Caroline: she was a very attractive lady who dressed expensively, spoke eloquently and came from a well-to-do area. Perfect. The only thing we had in common was that our offices were on the same street, and that there was a letter T in our surnames, which wasn't really enough for me to use as grounds to ask her out. But I really fancied her and thought that the deed should be done even though she was way out of my league. During one of our leisurely strolls to catch the bus, as expected it started to rain: a normal summer's day in Belfast. I suggested that we stop off in a café to prevent her from ruining her perfectly styled hair or soaking her fine clothing and I was amazed when she agreed. She asked for a coffee to which I obliged and offered the cup to her across the table. The contrast between her dainty manicured digits and my grubby oil-caked fingernails was glaringly obvious. After that my hands stayed in my pockets out of sight until further needed. Gazing into her blue eyes, I listened as she babbled on about handbags; makeup etc, all the while convinced she had no interest in me at all so why would I make a fool of myself by asking her out. While she was rambling on about her perfect life I foolishly suggested that we go out on a date and foolishly she said yes. My stunned blank look went unnoticed as I stared into her eyes for a few minutes before recovering from the shock. This was new territory for me as I'd never taken a nice girl out in full public view before: usually it was down to the Social Club with a *dirt bird*. My inexperience in this department was apparent when I asked her to accompany me one evening to the Loyalist Club instead of a quiet, romantic lounge bar. She was initially against going up there, essentially because it frightened her and also because the Shankill was not a place that was top of her shopping list but she agreed after I convinced her she would be safe. Saturday arrived and I was both nervous and excited about taking Caroline out, though I did think it might have been a big mistake to choose the Loyalist Club. This was a girl who had led a very sheltered life and who had had very little experience with the riff-raff from the other side of town.

With the song *Magic* by Pilot playing on the radio in the background it was time to head out the door to meet her. I paused for a glance in the mirror and thought, *How could she not fancy me?* I was dressed like a *dog's dinner*: a beige shirt, collar carefully spread out over the lapels of my best brown jacket; pure white parallel trousers ending an inch above the ankles; and to top it all off black socks and a pair of gleaming black Oxford shoes ready for action. We met at the city hall and began our amorous stroll to the club. It was a warm summer's evening and construction was in progress on one side of the Shankill Road so we chose to walk on the opposite side that was lined with derelict houses. As we passed the rundown buildings, four kids – all young girls about 10 years old – jumped out to obstruct our path. They were filthy street urchins with large white eyes peering from their blackened faces. I moved my arm across Caroline's body to protect her from an imminent attack by the young ragamuffins.

"*Clear off,*" I shouted bravely, awaiting appreciation from my lady friend for showing no fear in front of these waifs. Before we could move on one of the more dangerous looking girls confronted me, stopping any further movement up the road. She looked right into my face and bellowed, "*You're my cousin, you're my cousin!"* and jumped up and down in front of us as we tried to pass.

"No I'm not, go away!" I replied, grasping Caroline's hand and preparing to cross the road.

"Yes I am, yes I am, I`m Sandra!" she kept on shouting as she ran round and round in circles. We reached the other side with Caroline questioning me about what had just happened as I tried to explain that she had just been some crazy street kid. I had realised that it was my cousin when she had called out her name but there had been no way of recognising her under all that dirt and Caroline certainly was not going to find out that we were related. It was dark now so I used the situation to hold Caroline close as we passed the roadside construction. None of the street lamps were working, which made it difficult to see the dimly lit barriers that surrounded the large freshly dug construction holes in the road. I looked back to see that our diminutive assailants were away in the distance and so I knew it would be safe to cross back over.

"Be careful, don`t be frightened, hold my hand as we are crossing," I said gallantly. My arm flailed behind, searching for her delicate fingers as we moved out into the street. Then all of a sudden: splat!

"*Arggg! Help, shite, what happened*?" I had fallen into one of the construction holes! Right into a dark, wet, slimy crater in front of my true loves very eyes. Then I heard her soft puzzled voice speak out as she searched for an answer to my sudden departure.

"*Alan, where are you, are you ok?*" Looking up from my bunker and seeing her confused pretty face I assured her that everything was fine as I attempted to crawl up to street level. My earlier carefully-measured coolness had by now been totally blown away as I emerged from my misfortune thankful that she had not taken the plunge as well. She stepped back a few paces to avoid contact with me as if in fear of catching an infection from something that might have been dragged back from the hole. My pure white parallels were now mud brown as were parts of my shirt and face; I had to get to the club to try and clean myself up. Not much was said between us during the final 10 minute walk up the road as she seemed to have been slightly stunned by the recent events. I'm sure she hadn't had many first dates comparable to this one as the look of confusion and disbelief on her face was evident. Just as we were arriving at our destination a few red lights could be observed ahead of us; they seemed to be moving. As we got closer, two swaying drunks were singing and dancing with traffic cones on their heads and carrying lit up signs that said Danger: Road works ahead. *Hmm...I* thought. *It all makes sense now.*

How would my pretty thing react to all this disorder? It looked like it was all over bar the shouting. I tried to scrub up in the club but soap and water only made the stains worse. My next hour was spent standing up or walking about until my clothes dried off. The exaggerated movements along with the brown patches on my trousers gave me the appearance of a man who had just shit himself. As I waddled around the room Caroline was rapidly losing interest in me and seemed very uncomfortable with being surrounded by gangsters and gunmen, not to mention with *The Crystal Chandelier* and *Rhinestone Cowboy* being constantly played by the resident country and western band. She eventually decided that it was time to get out and requested a taxi to take her away from the assorted lowlifes. We left together and that was it: our relationship was over. We saw each other from time to time at work but she would smile at me then walk on by.

Whilst walking along close to the Loyalist Club one Saturday afternoon with Colin and Sammy the distinct sound of a machine burst was heard and automatically we scrambled to seek cover. The club had been a target for a number of attacks and another one was occurring: this time two men standing on a street corner had been wounded in the legs from a drive-by shooting. Minutes later we arrived at the scene of the hit to see a crowd that had instantly gathered, some of them distressed and aiding the two wounded men who were lying in a pool of blood. Others were raging, rushing around with obvious revenge on their minds. We had arranged to meet some of our ex-workmates from the GTC for a reunion drink but it now seemed like a bad time for it to happen and the day was not about to get any better. Inside the five *eejits* we were to meet were already there having a drink; they had been signed in by Colin's girlfriend. None of them had been to the club before which unfortunately turned out to have consequences later. One of the lads – a country boy we called Farmer – got involved in an altercation with a few local Shankill boys. He jumped up to confront one of them and pulled a belt with a large silver buckle from his jeans and began swinging it above his head. It was a big mistake. Sammy, Colin and I were at the bar when someone advised us to go into the main hall as there was a serious issue occurring there involving one of our friends. The commotion was made apparent by the shouts and squeals that were echoing along the hallway. As we entered the other room Farmer was being dragged towards a fire exit, taking a barrage of blows to his head and body, which were causing blood to squirt from his battered nose. Our other four friends were standing motionless and watching the beating, too frightened to intervene until they saw us rush to Farmer's aid. Then it was a free for all: tables and chairs were upended, sending glasses and bottles flying; punches rained in from all directions; and once again I got a bottle over my head. The riot finally stopped when one of the top UDA men began yelling for all involved to stop and tapped the inside of his jacket in order to indicate that he was packing heat. The threat of retribution in the form of a kangaroo court appointment soon ended the brawl. We helped Farmer into a taxi then on to hospital to get stitched up. I also had a couple stitches myself to close up my head wound. The country boy had got entangled with city stuff that he hadn't known how to deal with, and he had paid the price.

The club was becoming more like the Wild West and was a dangerous place to be entertained so I decided it was best to stay away for a while: there were too many crazies around. The Shankill area had always been a tough place with all sorts of characters: some friendly, funny people to go along with the mentally unstable. One of the loose cannons happened to be the brother of Sammy's girlfriend Roz, a person that Wee Jim and myself had the misfortune of meeting one evening at a bar on the Shankill Road. Sammy worked in the pub and came outside with us during his break. A car pulled up beside us with a disturbed passenger shouting at us to get in. Jim and I looked puzzled but Sammy advised us to get into the car, which we did; the driver then accelerated around a corner to stop suddenly in an alleyway. The passenger was Roz's mental brother, Walter, and he was completely *blootered*. He turned his mental head, stared with crazed eyes and questioned us.

"OK Sammy, who are these two?" His face was twitching uncontrollably as he glared fiercely at us. Sammy explained who we were, and then Walter carried on.

"Great, two more will be better, we're leaving tonight." Again Jim and I turned to each other, both baffled; then Sammy asked him what he was on about. Walter grabbed a bag from the floor and opened it to reveal a couple of handguns.

"We're heading down to the border tonight to set up camp, then we'll take out any IRA men coming across, they'll never know what hit them," he mumbled animatedly. Jim and I never spoke a word the entire time we were in the car but we knew something had to be done in order for us to get out of the mad scene that was evolving. Jim elbowed

Sammy in the ribs in an effort to try and make him come up with something to save us from the unhealthy situation that was occurring so Sammy responded shakily.

"Ok Walter but first take us back to the pub and we'll grab my mate's van; we'll need some provisions like beer and food to keep us going and we'll catch up with you later." Crazy Walter hesitated then fell for it insisting that we needed to pick him up a couple of bottles of scotch. We got to the pub, went out the back door, then began running and didn't stop until we reached the city centre. Each of us stayed in our own area for the next few weeks and thought it would be better to stay off the Shankill. Apparently Walter was so drunk he forgot about even seeing us that night which was a relief as we expected he would turn up at our doors at any time. It is unknown if he ever succeeded at the border.

I'd managed to get two more mates from the estate a job with me in the lift company on Donegal Pass which was great for travelling together. Each Thursday we'd get paid then go for a drink in either the Augalee or the Klondyke pub in Sandy Row before heading home. When I first started the workers met in the Crown Bar, where both Catholics and Protestants could drink together because of its secure city centre location. Although the pub was pretty safe from any religious aggravation, it was situated exactly opposite the Europa Hotel – the most bombed hotel in the world – so there was always a chance of being blown to smithereens. The problem with meeting at the Crown was that the vans could not be left unattended in the city centre because of the bomb threat so the engineers would leave an apprentice in the van and bring the drinks out to them. They would change over after a couple of pints to give each a chance to sit in the pub. I'd been in a minivan for my second sitting outside and after my workmates had had about four pints I was cold and bored stiff so I started it up to stay warm and began messing around with the gears. Suddenly the van sped backwards, stuck in reverse; then it smashed into a parking meter. I ran into the pub in a panic to get the driver, Mad Mick, before the army came to blow it up; he flung me into the van and raced away from the pub leaving a bent and crumpled parking meter in our wake. I thought that Mick was going to kick the shite out of me for being such a plonker but all I got was very a severe bout of verbal abuse. We had to change pubs after that.

We moved on to Moses Hunter's (locally known as Mosey Hunter) just around the corner from the office. My mum warned me not to go to the pub after being paid because I had blown all of my wages the week before in the Crown – but I figured one pint wouldn't hurt. Besides, she'd never know. As soon as I walked through the doors of the pub I heard,

"Croft, does your ma know yer here, don't go blowin' yer hard earned wages again, away home wi' ye." Looking over to the corner, I saw three of my uncles; John, Jim and Willie sat chuckling away. I was *scundered*. They were known to wander the town drinking in various pubs and unluckily for me they were in Mosey Hunter's. I had one pint and cleared off home.

That was the reason we chose to drink in the Augalee or the Klondyke after work as my uncles didn't go into Sandy Row much; however Catholics wouldn't go there either because it was in a staunch Protestant area. Most of the locals split their time between each bar and we got to know the different characters well and have a great old *craic* with them. One evening we grabbed our wage packets and headed over to the pub; this particular night we met in the Augalee. We could have easily chosen the Klondyke but by chance we didn't and if we had done who knows what direction our lives may have taken. It started off much like any other night with a crowd from the Albion works and Murray's tobacco factory sharing a jovial pint and a game of cards. The old lady with a half lit cigarette hanging from her mouth doing her regular drunken dance to the cheering audience. Things were all right in the Augalee as they probably were in the Klondyke; people were innocently having fun.

Suddenly an explosion tore through the night, instantly silencing the singing and background music as the merriment was shattered along with the stained glass that rained down upon us. People began screaming, some bleeding from the scattered glass shards that had become embedded in their heads and limbs. After the initial shock we realised that there was no further damage – no smoke no walls blown in – but the shrieking from nearby was bone-chilling. Looking through the splintered window frames we could see that the Klondyke had been hit: one main wall was missing and we could see several dusty, powder-covered figures amongst the debris staggering in shock, as well as others lying motionless. The lucky ones walked to the street moaning, speechless, crying or wailing. My instant reaction was to run to the smouldering building; I was unaware that the roof and adjacent supporting wall were beginning to crumble and were ready to collapse. It was an instinctive response to the aftermath of the deadly attack and I was not alone: others had rushed to the aid of the wounded without thinking of their own safety. The initial entry across that threshold will stay with me forever; everything that happened next I can relive in precise and accurate steps. Although it was a chaotic sight – sirens wailing, people scrambling over the rubble, shouting and sobbing for assistance – to me it was silent and in slow motion. I felt like I'd entered the stage of a play in a hazy dreamlike scene. The long wooden bar was almost intact with an old man still standing at it mumbling incoherently in his singed and tattered clothing. Towards the back wall a section of the bar had buckled, and was now lying across the waist of a trapped man; only his arms, head and chest were visible and he was groaning in agony. Someone called out frantically to those around.

"Lift the bar up, we'll pull him out!" I remember a woman holding his hand, trying to comfort and reassure him as he drifted in and out of consciousness. A few of us helped to move the splintered metal and wooden structure up so the others could extract the suffering man below. When we lifted the bar time seemed to stand still. I was unprepared for what I was about to see and an adrenaline rush surged through me as I nearly passed out. The poor man had nearly been cut in half and as they pulled, his body separated and then he died; the weight of the bar had been keeping him alive. Dazed, we slowly lowered the twisted frame back to the ground after his body had been fully removed; then the remains were covered with jackets and coats. I walked further into the bar where I found a woman weeping, crouched on the floor and hands covering her head. She rose silently to grasp my hand; then I escorted her out to the street as I tried to avoid the sharp twisted debris protruding from all angles. The fire brigade had arrived and began ordering everyone to get away from the bar as it was about to cave in. The impulsive amateur aid workers had now become a hindrance to the emergency services and were preventing them from getting their equipment into the building.

Slowly I began to comprehend what had just happened. The police started to cordon off the area in order to separate the scene from the crowd that had gathered and the people who were curiously pushing against the barriers. Although standing amongst a crowd of people I felt completely alone. I had been numbed by the incident. I turned around and I sighted Big Stevie leaning against a wall, shaking and vomiting. This big tough hard man had had his soft centre exposed and he had been brought to his knees. I watched him for a moment then walked away. The mates who I'd earlier been laughing and drinking with were somewhere within the police barriers but had been lost to me amidst the disarray. Most of what happened after watching Stevie's breakdown is a blank; the next thing I remember I was back at home sitting on the sofa. As I sat shaking and shivering in my mum's arms shock set in. She made me a cup of tea and wrapped a blanket around my shoulders. Someone died that night and countless were injured or maimed, all for the glorious cause. It would be one of the most traumatic experiences of my life.

A few months went by before I ventured into the city centre. I felt myself getting more and more incensed as I approached 18 and I was starting to act recklessly; things were only made worse by events that followed. A bomb blast on the Shankill Road killed one more of my mother's cousins and a few months later another relative was murdered; he was found west of the city, shot in the head in a sectarian killing. After these events a few of my mates and I would go head to head with our Catholic foes in certain areas, always making sure that we outnumbered them. One of us would usually go over to shout abuse at any crowd that was loitering about and when they gave chase the rest of us would jump in and slap them about. One time it backfired on us when we took on more than we could handle and ended up getting cornered in the Unity Flats area. Colin, Sammy, his cousin Paul and I began abusing a couple of clowns who were standing in an alleyway wearing Celtic shirts; they took the bait and were ready for a scrap. When they approached we went in for the kill but Colin fell over as we ran towards them and when we stopped to help him a mob of about seven or more surrounded us. A few of them were carrying their favourite weapon – the hurley stick – and began pounding us as we ran for safety towards a wall that led to the lower Shankill area. Before we climbed the wall we took a good beating with Paul coming off the worst, suffering a laceration to the back of his neck by a broken bottle. We survived but only just; if we hadn't been close to the wall we would have likely ended up in hospital or dead.

Since my last skirmish on the Shankill I thought I'd try a pint or two in a more relaxed and somewhat safer location. The Harland and Wolff (H&W) club backed onto Queen Street in the city centre; as the name suggested, most of its membership was made up of people from the shipyard (H&W). It was separated from Romano's nightclub by a large fence topped with barbed wire. Romano's was a trendy club that was frequented almost exclusively by Catholics; this was the reason for the fence, as the H&W club clientele was all Protestant. At the end of the evening as the two sets of punters emerged I learned that a running battle was sometimes on the late night menu. Missiles – mostly beer bottles – were hurled over the fence and if you were not prepared it was easy to get a direct hit on the head.

One night after the club closed Sammy and I got separated from the usual crowd we went home with and we soon found ourselves face to face with some stragglers leaving Romano's. At that time it was possible to tell a Catholic from a Protestant by the way they dressed and they had our number immediately. We knew who they were and we began to make a run for it but they managed to catch up with us near the old Smithfield bus station which was in a very poorly lit Catholic area. Before we could get a blow in we were on the ground getting kicked and punched by about five of them who were clearly enjoying themselves. It looked like we were done for as we assumed the fetal position to try and absorb most of the damage but they were not letting up and there seemed to be no way out. Then we heard:

"Right, you lot stop if you know what's good for ye."

The crowd halted, hesitated, then scattered as quickly as they had arrived. I looked up; my vision blurred from the blood streaming from my face, and saw a dark shadow leaning on a black taxi with a gun in his hand. He glared at us with disdain and snarled:

"You two, get up and clear aff, you got lucky tonight!"

We struggled to our feet and laboured up the road as fast as our aching bodies could move. We were indeed lucky: the gunman had been a taxi driver for the IRA that for some reason had taken pity on us. After that I once again gave the city centre a wide berth, preferring the mundane existence and relative safety of the estate. Sammy decided to spend more time with his girlfriend even though her brother was a raving loony and on top of that her ex-boyfriend, another psycho, was threatening him with death for no apparent reason.

My dad had agreed to lend me the money to buy a car in an effort to keep me on the straight and narrow and hopefully away from Sandy Row and the Shankill. For 100 pounds I picked up a gem: a 1964 Wolseley Hornet that was really a mini with a sticky out boot and a nice walnut dashboard. It felt great to be on the road again after my unfortunate motorway experience and I enjoyed cruising around the area waving to all the girls. The chick magnet worked but unfortunately most of my lady friends were a couple of shillings short of a pound. When I asked one girl if she fancied going to the pictures with me to see *One Flew Over the Cuckoo's Nest* she declined admitting that she had a limited knowledge of birds and did not want to sit in an audience of intellectual ornithologists.

On one drive to Carrickfergus I picked up an old mate from school, Davy A., who had been standing in the rain at a bus stop. He was known as Davy A. to distinguish him from Davy B. and Davy C, all who were in my class at school. It was because of this encounter I was to meet Vicki who would become my first steady girlfriend. She lived opposite Davy and called him over when we arrived at his house to ask for a favour; then she invited us both in. I was taken by her posh educated accent and was surprised to see an immaculate interior to her home. It seemed a bit out of place for a council house. Her mother was having a problem with the kitchen sink so Davy and I agreed to help. When she slinked into the living room I had to step back in disbelief. Vicki was a good looking girl but her mother was a stunner: long blonde hair and a body of a 21-year-old. Later at Davy's house I asked how these two elegant women had ended up living in a shithole council estate. He told me that they had fallen from grace and were now penniless, living off the government and housed by the council. Vicki was the daughter of a famous Irish tenor and although I had not heard of him Davy assured me that he was famous and pointed out the large LP collection in his name. Apparently the old warbler was a bit of a boy and had several kids but unfortunately Vicki did not get much attention from him. Vicki invited me back to her place again and not long after that I asked her to go out with me, to which she agreed. I didn't have the nerve to ask her mother out. Vicki had an innocence about her which I found pleasing. We'd been going out for about three months, and we'd been having fun and staying out of trouble when a bit of bother occurred. The rabble from Vicki's housing estate disliked anyone connected to the mob from my estate and vice versa. I was aware of this and kept my visits low profile though one of the so-called hard men had been watching my movements and decided to let me know I was not welcome there. Just as I was leaving one night a shadowy character came up from behind and stuck something into my back as I opened the car door, then said:

"I know who you are, get in the car we're going to do a wee job and you're

going to be the driver."

I looked round to see a well known local head case behind me with his hand in his pocket as if he was holding a gun. He was drunk so I thought it was a wind-up and that he was pretending to be James Cagney or something but I knew he had connections so I had to be careful. We stood staring each other out waiting to see who would make the next move when thankfully I heard Davy A.'s voice.

"Oi, McKane, what's your problem, clear away aff,"

"What's it got to do with you?" He replied and turned to confront Davy.

"He's my mate; do ya want to make something off it?" Davy threatened, clenching his hands into fists. McKane mumbled some profanities then walked away. Davy said that he was not sure if my wannabe hijacker carried a gun and that although he had connections he was not well-liked on the estate. It was then that I found out that Davy was in the UDA; unfortunately he would end up in jail a year later. Vicki and I stayed together for another month and although I had to put up with a bit of occasional abuse from the locals that was not the reason we split up. She had a very good heart but seemed to be a little girl lost with mixed emotions and fantasies of grandeur: she hoped to be a singer one day like her dad. We were from different worlds and Vicki had fallen out of hers into mine: one she did not belong in. Sometimes when we were alone in a cosy intimate setting she would suddenly break out into song: *For the Wings of a Bird,* etc. Strange days indeed. It was time for me to move on.

I had never gone out with any girl for more than a week until I met Vicki; then after we split I was in another relationship within a month. A popular alternate night spot on a Saturday was in the costal town of Bangor in County Down. Transport was a must for this destination so with my trusty Wolseley Hornet I and a few others began to frequent this locale every weekend. We would meet up with Colin and Sammy along with their girlfriends in a club called the Queens Court, right on the seafront. It was a bit of posh joint, dimly lit with candles on the table and a bar that encircled the dance floor where you could buy exotic liquors such as Cinzano and Quantro. One evening I arrived with Wee Jim and managed to squeeze into an alcove with Colin, his girlfriend Janet and another girl. John had no problems with the ladies: they usually asked him out so I thought he'd snap up the pretty girl at our table. She was blonde – very attractive – and by the way she talked she sounded like she was a local girl. Jim went to the bar so Colin and Janet introduced me to Ally as I smiled and did my best James Dean. At that time most of us had long hair and smoked a lot; I acted cool by picking up a candle to offer Colin a light as he put a cigarette to his mouth while conversing with his girlfriend. I tapped him on his shoulder and he turned into the flame and ignited the hair on the left side of his napper. *Whoosh*, with the smell of burning rubber he was half bald in milliseconds and if it wasn't for Janet's quick thinking as she extinguished it with a pint of lager he would have been a Mexican hairless. Glancing over at Ally still with the candle in my hand I could see she was not impressed. Janet was more pissed off than Colin was though he never left the alcove for the rest of the evening and kept his half scorched head away from public viewing. Jim cleared off with a bit of stuff he'd picked up and by the end of the night I somehow found myself alone with Ally. She accepted my offer of a ride home and that night agreed to see me again the next week; then we began seeing each other regularly. I was driving down to see her a couple of times a week for the first month when one night I was approached by two hoods that lived close by. One of them put his hand on my chest to stop me and said:

"I've a message from Shooter, he says if you don't stop seeing Ally you'll need a new pair of knees."

Shortly after Ally and I discussed my friendly little encounter with the local delivery boys and I asked her to explain the Shooter connection. They had been going out together for about 10 months but Ronald – aka Shooter – had had a run-in with the army while he had been carrying a couple of guns in his car and had been sent down for two years. He had not accepted it when she had broken up with him and had kept sending her letters from prison, including a recent one informing her that he would be out on parole soon. That was all I needed: another psycho to deal with. I really liked Ally and didn't want to split up with her but the threats kept coming: first notes on my car notifying me of his imminent return; then somebody slashed one of my tyres.

I spoke to my sister's boyfriend Big Jim and told him what had been going on with Ally and me and asked him if could find anything out about this so called Shooter who resided at Long Kesh Prison. Within two weeks Big Jim called to inform me that it was all sorted and that I would not hear from this Shooter person again and that if I did then he'd finalise it, whatever that meant. There were advantages of knowing people in unsavoury high places even though they were the types of places to steer clear of. However, my relationship with Ally only got worse after Shooter was finally released. He approached her one night at a bar we were in but totally ignored me; I only found out that he was the infamous Shooter after he'd left. He had been about five foot nothing and had looked like a gerbil. So what other secrets had Ally been keeping back from me? Apparently she'd been shagging about at 17 and had got up the *duff*; it turned out that her baby sister was in fact her daughter and the child's mother was in fact the wicked grandmother. Ally and I stayed together for over six months but all things must pass and eventually she gave me the boot. I never liked her ma anyway.

Once more I was single and free to make bad decisions again which usually resulted in me getting a smack in the mouth somehow. I was hanging around with some unsavoury characters and generally drinking too much. Sammy and Roz had announced that they were going to get married and this had been followed up by Roz's crazy ex-boyfriend announcing that he was going to shoot Sammy if the wedding went ahead. I had got a phone call from the somewhat happy couple informing me that they were postponing the ceremony but not the wedding. They had booked a flight to England and would be getting married in Manchester later that month. With the sound of *I'm Going to Barbados* by Typically Tropical playing everywhere, arriving in rain swept Droylsden in Greater Manchester was a bit of a comedown. A total of 12 people attended the wedding – the bride and groom; Sammy's mum and brother with a few relatives; me the best man and Wee Jim the bridesmaid. They began married life living in a car of a family friend in Manchester; eventually they returned to Northern Ireland to live in the countryside somewhere.

Being best man at Sammy's wedding was a strange and stress-free event but my next appearance in this role was quite the opposite: Billy had decided to take the plunge into the unknown and had asked if I would be his best man and of course I had said yes and I was terrified. He was married at the local Presbyterian Church; then it was on to a reception in Carrickfergus where the congregation awaited the festivities and speeches. I sat at the bar knocking Bacardi's down my neck in order to try and raise my Dutch courage. Apart from Billy's family the rest of the crowd were unknown to me: her family were from Scotland and outnumbered Billy's by about three-to-one. His new wife had no time for his friends or me – hence the lack of us at the wedding – but she could not stop me from attending as I was the best man and that really pissed her off. Finally the time had come for my speech. I'd downed a bottle of Bacardi by then but was still stone cold sober as I stood quivering with the thank you cards in my hand as I faced an audience of strangers. The first card I chose had me double-checking the wording as it seemed that either my eyes were beginning to play tricks on me or it was in a foreign language. "*Lang may yer lum reek,*" was on the card so I read it aloud even though I didn't know the meaning. A large applause rippled around the room in appreciation of my delivery and I waved to the assembly with gratitude for their acceptance of my profound oration, which I was completely baffled by. The remainder of my speech was adlibbed and a lot easier following my attempt to speak Scottish and I was later informed that the card had meant *"long may your chimney smoke"* – or have a long and prosperous marriage.

Before we had gone to England for Sammy's wedding, a school friend, Tommy, had called to ask if I knew any of the Sandy Row paramilitaries and if I could take him there as he wanted to join up. He had tried to convince me to also join as the Troubles were not going to end any time soon and we would be fighting for the cause and gaining respect from our peers. I had said I'd think about it and that I'd let him know after we returned from the wedding. Sammy and Roz having had to leave because of a couple of crazies had had me contemplating how these people should pay for their evil actions and I had begun thinking that maybe joining up would give me the power to do so. Upon return I called to arrange a meeting with Sandy Row but Tommy said he'd already signed up with the local brigade. I was relieved not to have to go through with the senseless idea and with that any thoughts of me getting involved quickly disappeared. Apparently Tommy had been sent to perform a drive-by hit of an innocent Catholic but had purposely missed the shot as the car had gone by. The police had got the vehicle description and had had him and the driver in custody in a matter of days. Eventually he was charged with attempted murder and was sent down for 10 years.

Reports were that prison life was hard on him as he suffered retribution from his own kind when they found out that he had had no intention of carrying the hit out. Tommy had had a quest for glory that had ended in heartbreak and misery for his family and himself but it made me think about how close I had been to being in his shoes. Tommy's desire to get involved had been a real surprise to me: he was a quiet and unassuming kid who had somehow chosen to go over to the dark side. He was just one of the many who did.

Once again I decided to stay close to home and began to partake in a drink in the somewhat placid surroundings of the local Social Club. It was a small metal structure with a main hall for entertainment featuring a band that always played country and western music. My mates and I spent most of the time in the undersized, smoky back room playing pool. This was the only attraction of the club; the chances of pulling a woman were slim as most of them were married and hitting 50. One evening during a band intermission the building was rocked by an enormous bang. We could hear drum cymbals rattling along with people screaming. Instinctively we ran from the pool room to see a large smoking hole in the back wall and band equipment scattered around the room: a bomb had gone off at the rear of the club. Luckily no one was badly injured: mainly small cuts and bruises along with a lot of panic. The worst injury was to the man nearest the stage that had unfortunately ended up with the bass drum wrapped around his head. If nothing else we were freed from the racket of *The Crystal Chandelier* and *Rhinestone Cowboy*, along with other infuriating country and western songs. It was evident that even quiet non-sectarian clubs were now a target; this had been a small bomb left outside the building but it could have been lethal if it had been planted inside – we got lucky that night. After that incident we organised our own security system and took turns in patrolling the perimeter of the club, armed with a torch.

A pattern was emerging: that of young teenagers going to prison as a result of their blind involvement with the paramilitaries doing *wee jobs* consisting of robbery or worse. A few of these teenagers were good friends of mine who had totally messed up their youth. One morning as I drove to work with my mates we witnessed an armed man running up a road to an awaiting motorbike. Traffic was stopped by the commotion as another armed man lay flat across a stationary car's bonnet and aimed a pistol at the motorbike. He yelled warnings instructing the other man to stop but the bike sped off with him following their movement in his sights. Luckily no shots were fired as it could have been a disaster with the possibility of innocent people being hit. We later found out that the man who had been leaning on the car had been an off-duty police officer who had held back from opening fire. The gunman on the motorbike was known to us and had just murdered a Catholic at his workplace. We had all witnessed the incident but none of us had any intentions of going to the police to grass him up; it just was not the done thing. He was arrested for the crime a couple of months later and was sentenced to life, at only 18 years old.

With sectarian fighting and killing taking place under the somewhat false pretence that it was all about religion, certain events took place that proved that it didn't matter if you were a Catholic or a Protestant: evil people did evil things. My cousin Marian, six months older than me, was to find this out almost at the cost of her life. While walking home from a club one night with a casual male acquaintance she suddenly became subject to an unprovoked frenzied attack by this so-called friend, who battered her petite frame so gravely that she was left unconscious to die in an alleyway. If it hadn't been for an old woman investigating what she had thought had been an animal moaning in distress she would have certainly passed away. He'd punched and kicked her so ferociously there were boot mark treads on her face and her ear had been torn off. She was rushed to the hospital in a coma with suspected brain damage. After my uncle had visited Marian in the intensive care ward he went looking for revenge – banging on doors of people that knew the reprobate responsible – but to no avail: he had vanished. The family was called together in an attempt to hunt the scum down but we were unsuccessful and eventually the UDA put a hit out on him. Wisely he handed himself in to the authorities and went to jail under police protection; he was later shipped off to England for his own safety upon release. As far as I know he escaped any retribution from the paramilitaries. My cousin never fully recovered from the traumatic ordeal. She was deafened in the attack and to this day won't go out by herself and still lives with her mum. Marian is an inspiration in overcoming adversity: she has a mouth like a truck driver, smokes like a trooper and is one of the funniest girls that I know. She has kept her sense of humour considering what she has been through.

Things seemed to be spiralling out of control with no end in sight to the conflict. One day, Davy C., a school friend, called me to ask if I wanted to meet him for a drink. His best friend was Tommy and he was dismayed by what had happened to him. Ironically we met in a club ran by the UVF, a place frequented by some of the most notorious hoods in the area. Davy C. hated what was occurring and suggested we get away from all the turmoil. We arrived at opening time and apart from one other patron we were alone and I remember *Don't Cry For Me Argentina* was playing on the jukebox. I'd never ever thought about leaving Belfast before mainly because I didn't think that I could ever leave the security of my home, particular my mother. But I was fed up with gang warfare, fighting in bars and not knowing if the next bomb would be the last so I thought that maybe what Davy was proposing was a good idea. Word spread of our plan and surprisingly six other people wanted to join us on our worldwide expedition. A banker was suggested to collect money from each person as we prepared for our trip to the unknown. That idea was quickly scrapped as there was the strong possibility that the keeper of the money would do a runner with the stash. The group of eight slowly became the group of three – Davy C., Wee Jim and myself – although our destination was still a mystery. It was early June and Jim came up with idea of heading to the south of France to pick grapes. It didn't take long for him to convince us that his idea was a good one, particularly when we were informed that all the beaches were full of topless women. That was it: we were going to San Tropez. Grapes, sun and tits – you just couldn't beat it with a big stick!

CHAPTER 7

In London

Finally the day had come: we were leaving the grey desolate land of Northern Ireland for the bright sunny shores of France. Our parents waved us a teary goodbye as we boarded the Liverpool boat with Jim's mum shouting a final warning to us:

"Watch out for the con men!" Sound advice indeed. The boat drifted out of Belfast Lough, leaving the giant shipyard cranes in her wake and us on board without a care in the world. We had no game plan or even any thought of how long we would stay away. Perhaps just the summer. First stop was at the bar for a couple of pints each then heads down on a bench for the night. A damp morning greeted us at about 5 a.m. as we were awakened by the sound of the great lift locks operating as the boat negotiated its way, eventually arriving in the Albert Dock by about 6.30 a.m. Armed with a bag each containing a few clothing changes and enough money to last us for less than a month we made our way to the

Liver building to catch a bus to the Lime Street train station. Our journey was carefully planned: change at Birmingham then catch the train to Dover for the evening ferry to Calais. Simple, what could go wrong? We passed the time playing cards then grabbed a quick bite to eat at Birmingham before changing trains to the coast. By the afternoon the smell of the sea was distinctive as we excitedly neared our destination. Suddenly, we heard the stationmaster's voice over the PA system.

"Next stop, Southampton!" I had read the wall map at Birmingham and did not recall that we were supposed to go through Southampton on our way to Dover but I didn't dwell on it as we were on the south coast somewhere. We knew there was a problem when the conductor instructed us to get off the train at Weymouth, which was the last stop.

"Where's Weymouth?" Jim asked. Davy and I shrugged our shoulders. We checked the map at the station platform to find we'd gone west towards Cornwall instead of east to Dover. We'd boarded the wrong train during the changeover.

"Now what?" I enquired, *"Our plans are already ballsed up!"* So we went for a pint to rethink.

In the pub we got talking to some locals who suggested a trip to the Channel Islands as tomato picking was very popular and well-paid. Although it didn't sound as exotic as grape picking in France, it was definitely better than going home – but we were really only going to San Tropez for the tits! The ferry to Guernsey didn't sail until the next morning so we had to stay in Weymouth overnight. The town was packed with holiday-makers who were there for the summer and with no rooms available that evening we decided to sleep in one of the beach shelters. Tucked in the corner of one of the shelters was a large tarpaulin which was a perfect cover to protect us from the elements of the stormy sea. We spread out in order to make sure that none of us rubbed any part of our bodies against each other. Davy was on his left side facing the corner, Jim lay flat on his back gazing at the ceiling and I was on my right side looking into the shelter. It was quite dark inside our sleeping quarters with only the far corner – which I faced – dimly lit by the flickering moon's glow on the rolling waves. Movement for us was almost impossible due to the weight of the tarpaulin and so we fidgeted around as we attempted to sleep. A short period of time into the evening a couple crawled into the shelter unaware of our presence under the dark cover in the opposite corner. I warned the other two of what was occurring and told them to be silent. The male lay on his back, and then the female positioned herself between his legs and lowered his jeans. With her head bobbing up and down like a fiddler's elbow she began performing oral sex on him. I whispered to Davy and Jim and gave them a blow by blow (no pun intended) account as she drove him into a frenzy. She worked on him for about 5 minutes then climbed on for a 10 minute ride, howling like a wolf in the moonlight. My two disturbed comrades were going nuts as they could not turn round to witness the free porn show because of the weight of the tarp. After the sex-crazed couple had satisfied each other they were up and away without even an inkling that they had been the stars of a sideshow consisting of three audience members: one appreciative and two very frustrated.

After a pleasant cruise we disembarked and were greeted by a beautiful summer's day in St. Peters Port, the capital of Guernsey. One of the locals in Weymouth gave us directions to a pub – the Jamaica Inn – where some of the tomato pickers gathered for a drink. Following a short walk from the harbour we could see the large wooden pub sign swinging in the breeze. We entered to find a cosy interior with a few regulars sitting at the mahogany bar. We pulled out a stool each and joined them. After ordering three pints I asked the barman who we would speak to about tomato picking. Barely raising his head he grunted,

"There's no work here, the seasons over, clear off back to where you came from."

"What ya mean, we were told to come here to find work," I replied. I'd barely finished my sentence when a big shovel-faced Neanderthal at the bar joined in:

"You heard him, drink up and leave." The missing link then stood up and gave us the evil eye, so we left.

Davy suggested we try another pub that had been recommended to us: the De La Rue on the main harbour front. But first we needed to get cleaned up so we booked into a bed and breakfast for the night. The only thing available was a room with one double bed but they still charged all three of us. After a bit of laundry – washing our socks and underpants in the sink and hanging them on the window frames to dry – we scrubbed ourselves down for a night on the town. The De La Rue was packed with mostly young people who looked somewhat upmarket, but unperturbed we began to use our Ulster charm on the ladies, to no reward. As we stood in the corner being totally ignored by the opposite sex three large chaps in their 20's approached us. One of them questioned us in a Belfast accent.

"I hear you're from Belfast, how old is your granny?" he said to me with menace in his eyes. Shrugging my shoulders as I looked to Davy and Jim, I replied:

"Don't know, maybe 74 or 75."

His two sidekicks got closer and growled at us together in rough Glasgow accents,

"He said how old is your granny!"

"I've already told ya, moron," I said, getting pissed off. That was a mistake on my part. One of them grabbed me by the neck and the others blocked Davy and Jim off, preventing them from coming to my aid. They were a lot bigger than us so we held back on the off-chance that we might get battered. The Belfast clown turned to us and said:

"You're all Fenians; get out of the pub before we do you in, no Catholics allowed."

Baffled by what had just happened we shuffled out of the bar. After getting out of Northern Ireland to leave the Troubles behind we had ended up intimidated in Guernsey by three nutters from Belfast and Glasgow – bloody typical! I later found out that the question about my granny's age was a code to ask what my Orange Lodge number was even though none of us were in the Orange Order. The things you learn.

The next day we each bought a bus pass and explored the island, stopping off at small inlets with beautiful beaches for a paddle or a swim. The sea was surprisingly warm compared to the waters around Belfast Lough. In the evening we spent the night at a disco close to our hotel, which was perfect to walk from if we got lucky with the girls.

We bopped the night away dancing to an array of classic tunes such as *Shake your Booty* by KC & the Sunshine Band and *Dance Little Lady Dance* by the magnificent Tina Charles. Regrettably the only attention we got was from a dispute with some of the local ladies when Davy found a handbag in the men's toilets. One of the girls claimed that he had lifted it from a table then removed the purse and money. A scuffle ensued, followed by a punch-up with the bouncers, and in the end the three of us were turfed out on our arses. Yet another eventful evening ruined as Davy protested on the disco's doorstep, pleading his innocence but to no avail. So we picked up a couple of bottles of cider and headed back to the room. The next morning we were rudely awakened by Jim attempting to reach his dry washing of socks and underwear that was hanging from the window frame. Being smallish he had tried to compensate for his vertical disability by standing on the radiator. First there was a cracking noise then a cry of despair as he went airborne, landing on the bed with the laundry across his head as the radiator tore away from the wall and sent water cascading across the room. Alarmed by the early morning call Davy and I jumped out of bed, scrambling to locate the stopcock on the radiator to stem the flow. Within minutes the hotel staff were banging on the door, demanding to know what the commotion was all about and to see what damage had been done. Upon entry the very irate boss man began screaming obscenities at the three of us who were now standing dripping wet clad in only our underpants. Our clothing, which had been hung up only minutes earlier, had been soaked along with our bags; we grabbed the driest thing available to try and look respectable. The management advised us to wait downstairs in the dining room until they had cleared the room up. As we watched TV in the lounge we were called to the main foyer where we were greeted by two members of the local constabulary. One spoke, threatening:

"Right you three grab your things and get into the van outside, we're taking you to the airport, there's a flight to London leaving at 2pm and you're going to be on it. Get off the island and don't come back."

"What have we done?" Davy questioned.

"Where do I begin? You were upsetting customers in the Jamaica Inn, started a fight in the De La Rue, stole a handbag at the Harbour disco and now you've wrecked the hotel room, all this in just two days, now shut up and get going," he answered.

We could not believe what was happening but we had no choice: they had already booked the flights to London so we were to be kicked off the island and barred from Guernsey. Our parents would be billed for all damages and expenses if we could not find the money within the next month. The police frogmarched us past other travellers as if we were mad axe-murderers, from the van into the airport and all the way to the awaiting plane bound for Gatwick.

So far our wee excursion had been a disaster. Now we were stuck in London with no idea what to do next and with very little money. An ethnic minority in a visitor advisory booth had informed us of the availability of two free week's bed and breakfast at a centrally-located hostel for all newcomers to the city. Firstly we had to make our way to Camden Town to sign on the dole. The place was packed with all sorts of characters, some signing on for the first time or other habitual free-loaders trying to avoid work. These eccentrics had invented elaborate former occupations as they pursued employment in their qualified field. There were concert pianists, shepherds, deep sea scaffolders, ski instructors and other wondrous skilled tradespeople, all waiting to be called upon when needed.

After a lengthy wait we received our vouchers for two weeks bed and breakfast at St. Mongo's hostel, an old Victorian building in Charing Cross, close to Trafalgar Square. It felt like we were on holiday as we took in the London landmarks and mingled with the tourists who were feeding the swarms of pigeons dive-bombing throughout the square. This all changed when we entered the hostel. The place stank of an unpleasant detergent that had been used to try and mask the smell of piss and vomit. A shifty looking Asian geezer handed us our bed numbers then informed us that we'd have to be quick if we wanted to catch lunch. On our way down to the main dining room in the basement I understood what he meant by *catch lunch* as we passed a discarded plate with its contents splattered against the wall. Someone had carefully positioned a fork into something hard that might have once been a potato. We joined the queue of what could have easily been a film shoot about a soup kitchen from the great depression era. There were bums and hoboes pushing each other around as they clenched their plates in their grubby hands and awaited the delivery of the finest slops provided. Chicken pie was on the menu but what we collected was hard to say: it was a gravy-like substance with what seemed to be the skin of some bird, perhaps chicken. We looked at each other, put the plates down on the table, then left the hostel in search of a burger joint.

We had discussed staying on in London but realised we needed jobs if we were to find reasonable accommodation. We considered our immediate future as we lazed about at the hostel in the large recreational area by the snooker table and television. As we were waiting to play pool a man with a heavy Glasgow accent entered and asked if anyone was interested in doing some jobs for him. Immediately a group of desperates, including us, approached him keen to join his workforce.

"What kind of work it is it?" someone from the back of the room enquired.

"You'll be nicking some cars for me, I'll see you all right, it pays well," he replied. Not the type of work we were thinking of and although the majority of the group turned away he still managed to find a couple of mugs that he could unlawfully employ. Later that night we made our way to the sleeping quarters: giant dormitories on two floors filled with rows of beds, each equipped with a small cupboard on one side. Luckily we had been placed together which made us feel somewhat secure. Throughout the night the sounds of wailing, groaning, arguing and swearing filled the air so we thought it would be better to sleep with one eye open. The next morning a long-time resident warned us not to leave our belongings there as they would soon disappear: thieves were constantly on the prowl. We came to an agreement to rent a left luggage locker between us at Euston station where we could get washed and showered in the new *superloos* that had just been opened. For the next two days we slept at the hostel

but we got washed and stored our stuff at Euston station. Jobs were readily available in London if you were prepared to work in the hotel industry but it was poorly paid and was close to slave labour. A driver and helper job was posted in the Evening Standard newspaper and although our knowledge of London was almost zero there was nothing to lose. Jim and I applied and we were asked to come in for an interview. Davy saw an ad for a trainee fireman and went off to see what the possibilities were of getting started there. We agreed to meet back at the hostel later on.

The company for the driving job was located at King's Cross on Swindon Street, just behind the train station. As we knew nothing about the streets of London I cut a tourist map from a brochure and taped it to Jim's back. The plan was for him to go in first with me just behind and if I was asked any questions about my street knowledge I'd glance over at his back for the answers – brilliant! Outside the office a Bedford Beagle van and a blue five ton Ford lorry were parked. I'd never driven anything bigger than a Triumph Toledo, which I had smashed up a treat, so the Beagle would be no problem. The street was nonstop traffic which intimidated me a bit but I thought that I could handle it so with confidence we stepped in for the interview which went something like:

"How old are you?" It seemed like at trick question so I quickly added two more years on.

"21," I answered.

"Do you know London well?"

"Yes."

"Good, I'll give you a trial run around the block and if you're OK you can start on Monday, follow me."

As he rose from his chair Jim and I walked backwards away from his desk, allowing time for me to rip the map from his back before our cunning plan was exposed. We followed his fast-paced steps to the main street where he handed me the keys and pointed to the five ton truck and told me to get into the driver's seat. I looked at the Bedford van then back to the Ford lorry and just about shit myself. How could I possibly drive that huge truck? Jim waited while the manager held on as we circumnavigated King's Cross and I narrowly avoided everything moving or parked that came my way. Somehow we returned intact to the office without creating a major pileup. We exited the lorry and the manager said:

"You'll have to use your indicators sometimes but you done well, see you Monday at 7.30am."

He then hurriedly vanished through the front doors and into the building, leaving us standing bewildered on the roadside. We could not believe it:

we'd been in London two days and had managed to get work before we even had anywhere to live. Back at the hostel we played pool to pass the time, waiting for Davy to return from his job hunting exploits and excited about ours. Five o'clock, six o'clock, seven o'clock passed: no sign of him and he still hadn't returned by midnight. We weren't overly concerned about his whereabouts or if he was in any danger as at that age we felt like we were invincible and maybe the lucky bastard had pulled a woman.

The next morning his bed had not been slept in so we thought that he had definitely gotten lucky and had spent the night with some big blonde. Off we went on our trek to Euston Station for our daily wash at the *superloo* where Davy might possibly be waiting. Once again he did not show up but there was a cryptic message left for us at the left luggage locker. Inside were his key and a ticket receipt indicating that he had signed out; his clothes were gone and there was no note to inform us of where he was or where he was going? Also, the miserable bastard had cleared off with my good shoes, leaving me with the decrepit pair that I was wearing, soles flapping in the wind and my big toe sticking out of one of them. That was it for him: he'd mysteriously slinked away never to be seen again. Jim and I were on our own. We later found out from his family that he had made his way to New Zealand and was living with his brother. Davy had spent a year at sea school when he was 16 so when it was a no-go at the fire hall he had gone to the docks at Tilbury. There he had signed on at the merchant navy pool offices and had been able to join up with the crew of a boat sailing for New Zealand that night, with my shoes. He came back home within a year but eventually went back to New Zealand permanently.

Monday morning soon rolled round so we were bright and early for work, ready to fill in the relevant paperwork of employment. The insurance forms were completed showing my age as 21. It was a white lie that had to be perpetuated in order to advance my employment. The firm collected metal filing cabinets and desks from government buildings for restoration, and employed panel beaters and sprayers along with a few labourers. They were a right motley crew though one of the sprayers was a good lad; he also was called Alan and made us feel welcome. Our job was to go round London picking up damaged furniture to bring back for repair, which was later to be returned after refurbishment. Large filing cabinets were on our list the first day with a target to get to about eight different buildings. It was crazy: we were given the paperwork and went off into the unknown in this giant truck hoping to get to our destinations without killing anyone. Our new employer did not do much of a background or security check on us; otherwise we would have been shown the door pretty quickly. We felt like kings of the road taking all the wrong turns as we looked down from the cab of the lorry at all the mugs below. Jim shouted out the directions as I tried to follow the map but we seemed to go round in circles or go up one-way streets the wrong way. We made the first two pick-ups as we gradually got used to some of London's streets. The next building was at the back of Oxford Street and as we entered the building a shifty wee man emerged from the shadows of an adjacent doorway. He whispered to us:

"Who do you work for?" I looked around over my shoulder to make sure he was talking to me and said:

"James Casey and sons."

"I hate those bastards," he growled.

"Sorry to hear that mate but this is our first day and hopefully we'll get paid by him at the end of the week," I replied. He then asked:

"How much is he paying you?" Nosey bastard I thought, but what the hell.

"30 quid a week before tax."

"How many cabinets are you picking up from here?" he questioned.

John looked at the paperwork and told him there were two on the list.

"OK, take three instead of two and I'll give you 20 quid for the spare one," he said with a sinister grin. I ignored him and went inside. We were shown to a large storeroom with about 10 dusty old cabinets inside by a staff member who signed our sheet then left us to it. As we loaded the cabinets onto the lorry the wee man was still outside and stood in front of the lorry door to prevent me getting in.

"How many cabinets were in the room? I'll bet there were more than five or six. Go back for one more," he requested. I looked at Jim, hesitated slightly, and then went back for another. He loaded it onto the waiting van then handed us 20 quid. Before leaving he said:

"I'll see you again soon for the same deal." Then *whoosh,* he was gone.

Back at the office workshop all the cabinets were unloaded and made ready for repair, no questions asked. Our first day had gone relatively smoothly and we were 20 quid up before being paid. When the day was done we had to leave the lorry off at a large parking lot along with other company vehicles then pick it up in the morning. We had been at the hostel for a week by now and were ready to get out of it: the food was inedible and forget about trying to sleep – they'd steal the eyeball out of your head. It was a real cesspit. We moved out of the hostel to new accommodation. Our work lorry had blankets provided in the back to protect the freshly painted furniture and became our new sleeping quarters. We'd get to the office early and get washed inside the workplace before most of the staff arrived. The lorry was our residence for only a few nights before we found a room furnished with two beds in Highbury, close to Arsenal FC's ground. The club had failed to hit the same heights in recent years as they had during their dominance at the beginning of the decade with a memorable double year of league and FA Cup in 1971. The new place was about 20 minutes from work on the tube but it become expensive after a couple of weeks travelling back and forth. We decided instead of parking the lorry up for the night we'd drive it home to our new residence and leave it there overnight. What we didn't realise was that all parking spots were allocated by issue of permits for those who lived on that street. Some nights we were lucky; other nights not so lucky. We averaged about six parking tickets a month. Each one was flung in the bin.

We became good friends with Alan from work and we would meet up for a pint some nights after the day was done. He was an enigmatic character. He was about 10 years older than us, politely spoken and obviously very well-educated, and so we wondered why he was panel-beating and spraying old metal cabinets. As we gained his trust he revealed that he was working under an assumed name and that his real name was Paul. The government was after him for tax evasion and he stayed ahead of them by moving house, using an alias and changing jobs. Now the time had come for him to change it up again so he'd handed in his notice from work and was looking for somewhere to stay, and was hinting to us to put him up. One room with two single beds was not the perfect place to sleep three but he convinced us to let him move in and that he would not always be there.

Work was not the same without Alan/Paul and a new manager was giving us a hard time which seemed to coincide with my driving becoming more erratic. Previously some poor sucker had all but had his 1965 Ford Corsair destroyed at a roundabout in Aldgate when he had tried to sneak by on the inside lane then got crunched. Jim and I had got out seeing him pulling at his hair almost in tears: the wing of the car had been torn off and lay on the roadside with the headlight poking out like a huge dislodged eyeball winking at us.

"You've wrecked my car," he moaned.

"Ah shut up," I replied. *"It was your fault; anyway it's an old heap."*

With all the commotion going on and traffic being held up as people blared their horns a police constable came walking up.

"'*Allo, 'allo, 'allo, let's be 'aving you, what's all this then, who's at fault,*" he enquired. Both parties blamed each other and with a lack of witnesses the cop put his notebook away and walked off whistling the theme tune from *Dixon of Dock Green* after telling us to sort it out ourselves. With that we jumped into the lorry and took off, watching the irate loser jump up and down and wave his arms in the air from the wing mirror as we drove away.

Our next moment of madness and disorder happened at the exclusive Savoy Hotel just off the Embankment. Not knowing the hotel at all I arrived for pick-up at the front instead of at the tradesman's entrance to the rear of the building. The main driveway leading to the hotel was a dead end with the main foyer area having a small roundabout for cars to turn and drive back down and away. By the time I realised this we had driven the lorry right up to the atrium under the porch and I was unable to turn it around. The only way out was to reverse all the way back down the hill but it would be difficult because of all the high end cars parked on one side. Looking out of the side window, I could see a Rolls Royce, an Aston Martin, a Lotus and a few Jags to my left. I was worried about the potential demolition of the vehicles during the reversal and my only option was to run my right side wheels up onto the kerb of the foyer in order to gain the sufficient clearance to go back. Jim was to get out and direct me down the road to make sure the lorry was not about to hit anything. An audience had gathered to see what was literally an accident waiting to happen. Jim waved me back with the wheels up on the kerb, then *pop! smash! crash! bangle! dangle! banjo!*

"*Wow!*" Jim yelled, "*Look up!*" My head tilted sideways from the cab to see that the lorry's roof had taken out about six of the 15 or so decorative lights that hung below the atrium porch. The spectators were having fun and as I'd gone this far it would be selfish of me to spoil the show by stopping now. I summoned Jim to jump in and we carried on reversing, taking the remainder of the lights with us but being careful not to hit any cars. By now the concierge and some hotel staff had come out and had begun ranting and raving and shaking their fists at me as they avoided the shards of glass that were exploding from the large halogen lamps. Once we were clear of any obstacles we turned out from the hotel and onto to the embankment, then went full speed ahead, leaving enraged men in strange uniforms running behind us in futile pursuit.

My boss had been unaware of my trail of destruction, possibly because the truck was plain blue with no markings on it – but the next incident changed that. We were cruising down Holborn High Street with Jim snoring away as usual and me in a good mood singing *Desperado* by The Eagles as we sailed along. Up ahead on the left a van was parked with its back doors opened right out and around clipped to the side panels; the driver was delivering rolls of towels that were installed in bathrooms and toilets of pubs, etc. Adjacent to the van a car was in the outside lane indicating to turn right. My brain started computing distances, speed, time and if the gap between the car and the van was wide enough for me to take the five ton Ford through. What I had not allowed for was that the lorry side walls jutted out from the cab by about two feet, making the vehicle wider than the instantaneous calculations I'd come up with. Seconds later as I attempted the drive through, the left side of my truck caught the van's right back door and peeled the panel off like the lid of a tin of Fray Bentos corned beef. Next: pandemonium. The wing mirror swung into the cab, smashing Jim on the head and finally waking him up. Then the side of the van disintegrated into wooden particles that scattered into the air and floated down and landed like giant matchsticks. Spools of towel were catapulted outwards and upwards, unwinding like giant blue toilet rolls thrown at football matches, bouncing off walls and cars and causing pedestrians to do body swerves in order to avoid being swathed. Then I panicked and muttered in confusion:

"Jim, what'll I do? Should I keep going or stop?" He just sat there in shock; my head was spinning and the truck was in autopilot. We'd gone no more than 200 hundred yards when a black taxi swerved in front of us, forcing me to pull the lorry over to the side. Within moments he was joined by two other taxis that seemed to come out of nowhere. We were advised by members of the royal taxi police force to go back to the scene of the crime and discuss the situation with the van driver who was busily collecting his towel rolls. Later the real police came to sort the mess up and the incident was reported to my company. We drove to Highbury instead of going back to the office and went for a pint. Jim talked about packing the job in as sooner or later everything would catch up with us: the accidents, the filing cabinet caper and the pile of parking tickets that would eventually land on the firm's doorstep.

We thought about leaving London before the police caught up with us but we had no idea where to go. Paul advised us to get out of town for a while and suggested we take a trip to Hatfield with him to stay with a girl that he had used to go out with. He was never predictable so it wasn't much of a surprise when we got off the train at Enfield to visit an old friend of his that owned a panel-beating and car repair shop. After they exchanged greetings and a brown envelope for some car keys Paul took us to the back of the garage and pulled a tarpaulin from a dusty white 1969 Mercedes convertible sports car. With no questions asked Jim jumped into the passenger seat and left me to squeeze into the back. Paul started her up and we were on our way to Hatfield. We arrived at a large detached house that was neatly tucked away up a country lane where we were welcomed by a beautiful petite lady named Lisa who was dressed like something from the *Age of Aquarius* set. She offered us green tea and muffins then we walked around the grounds smoking some strange weed. Her husband had died about a year before in mysterious circumstances and since then she had lived alone; it was obvious that she was worth a few bob. We relaxed on the scattered beanbag chairs drinking wine and talking shite. Later Paul and Jim volunteered to drive and pick up some grub then hit the off-license to replace the booze we'd polished off. I stayed with Lisa to prepare for my haircut that we had agreed to earlier. She positioned me in a chair and started to merrily snip away at my high hair and before long I was listening to her life story. Born to rich parents who had never understood her (the usual old shite), she had become a rebel then had run away from home. Later she had met and married a captain in the paratroopers and had travelled the world but was now in a deep depression since he had been killed in some secret SAS pursuit. Then the waterworks began. She was blubbering and sobbing uncontrollably, snotters oozing from her nostrils as she recalled the great times they had shared together. I tried to console her by using some false sympathy, as I knew that she was quite vulnerable and that this was a perfect opportunity for me to take advantage of her. On and on she snivelled about her terrible existence, oblivious to the fact that I was even in the room with her. She could have as easily been talking to the Afghan coat hanging on the door. Then her arms became animated and began to flail about, resulting in the scissors narrowly missing my exposed right lug, flying across the room and then sinking into the sofa. Before I could calm her down she stomped out of the house and began running down the lane until she disappeared out of sight. Standing at the front door I began to think of the best way to explain what had happened when Paul returned. Walking back into the main room I lurched to a halt when passing the hall mirror. I looked twice at my reflection. The silly tart had only cut the right-hand side of my hair, leaving me like a half scalped Mohican. Eventually Lisa returned as if nothing had happened and we all got drunk. The next day she gave me some of her deceased husband's clothes that had been neatly stored in a macabre arrangement in the attic. One of the sweaters – with red white and blue hoops – fitted me perfectly and as a result I very rarely took it off; it became affectionately known as the *dead man's jumper*. Before we headed back to Highbury I had to pay for a repair job to my *barnet* which left me with a lot less hair than I had originally planned.

Paul had been staying with us full-time by now so it was becoming very cramped in the room. I had applied for another job but Jim was cheesed off and wanted to return to Belfast. Although things weren't so good at work or where we lived the nightlife was great; Paul knew a lot of people in the music business and took Jim and I to some great venues. We went to the Speak Easy on Margaret Street where we hobnobbed with Ritchie Blackmore and his wife. We got free entry to the Hope and Anchor in Islington to see the resident band, The Stranglers – all the while pretending we were in the music business. We met Chris Farlowe (famous for *Baby You're Out of Time)*, while we were hanging out at a close by Nazi memorabilia boutique where we dressed up and strutted around like German storm troopers. Paul claimed to be a one-time guitarist with *Hawkwind*, which would explain how he knew a few celebrities, and he had some great parties lined up for us to attend but Jim was losing interest fast. Things were a bit of a pain in the arse

ALAN CROFT

at night trying to get to sleep; plus we had all begun arguing a lot. I wrote to Billy, telling him everything was great apart from the accommodation, but I'm sure he could see through my world of pretence and that he knew I was not enjoying myself. A poem that he received from me summed up the situation and my state of mind at that time.

Alone in a room where three people sleep
My nightmare began in this rubbish heap
For two long weeks I've had to crawl
In and out avoiding the wall

The pressures of life all came to a peak
In such a place so dreary and bleak
But life's a gas, a poisonous gas
I think I'll lie down and crawl up my ass

Jim and I handed in our final notice at work and received the extra week's wages that we were owed. There was a possibility of us starting new jobs packaging and delivering clobber for a company in the rag trade on Old Street but Jim took his money and left.

Being alone was not easy but I was stubborn and didn't want to go back home to hear people yapping on about my failed adventure. Paul had started seeing more of Lisa so most of the time I hung around with a couple of older chaps who lived in same building. They were delivery men for Pickford's furniture company. One of them was a peculiar person with a slight Northern Ireland accent though he maintained that he was from the USA and that he had been in the bomber that had dropped the bomb on Nagasaki. Now he worked for Pickford's which to some might have seemed quite monotonous though I'm sure it was every bit as exciting as dropping nuclear bombs for a living. The other one had no teeth and farted a lot. But these were my new friends; it was them or no one.

My new job was shit: very little of it was on the road and most of the day was spent stuffing coats into plastic bags. The owner of the company was a miserable old Jew who treated the employees as second-class citizens; then again, some of them weren't even citizens, especially the ones who couldn't speak English. To release me from my endless boredom of bagging various garments I would purposely break the lift then volunteer to fix it, citing my previous experience in the trade. On one of the rare delivery trips a workmate of mine – the only Londoner – took me to the Blind Beggar pub on the Whitechapel Road and to Bethnal Green to see where the Kray twins had used to hang out. And I had thought Belfast was tough. My demise in the rag trade came when instead of doing the weekly hand washing and polishing of the boss's Daimler I decided to take it for a spin along to Moorgate and have a spot of lunch. Needless to say I received my marching orders upon return from my furious superior who exploded into a frenzy, going for my throat and swearing at me in Yiddish when I handed him a parking ticket.

I was out of work and slowly running out of money; then Paul disappeared off the face of the earth after a party we'd attended in Kensington. After he left the party I found myself surrounded by a gathering of musical hippie freaks who totally ignored me and I ended up being bored to death on the balcony by the lead singer of an Australian band Sherbet that had just hit the charts with the song *Howzat*. He kept telling me how great he was and how he would become rich and famous once he was the greatest lead singer of any band in England. Although he was the only one paying attention to me even I couldn't take it any longer and when he turned his back on me I pushed him off the balcony where he fell to his death. That's what I wanted to do but in fact I crawled over to a sofa in the corner of the living room and went to sleep. When I woke the next morning a bedraggled witch woman with long matted hair informed me that the red Lebanese hashish was on the table in the silver curio box and the scotch was in the decanter. Then she left. I got up and looked around to find there was no one else in the luxury Kensington apartment except myself so I went into the kitchen, grabbed a lump of smoked salmon, dumped the dope on the table and cleared off with the curio box.

Upon my return to Highbury I discovered that Paul had done a runner after he had been tracked down by the taxman so I made my mind up to go home. My parents were over on holiday at my aunt's in St. Albans so I decided to pack London in and head up there and travel back with them. The US air force bombardier owed me money and with only a fiver to my name I needed it for the train fare north so I went to his room to find him. The door opened slightly when I rapped on it and I called his name but I walked in only to find an old bearded bum asleep in his bed. Whoever he was I could not wake him; he was out for the count and smelt like a brewery, and was snoring like a chainsaw. When I went to the landlord to hand my key in I asked if he had seen my old friend from Pickford's, only to be informed that he had left to go back to the USA. I thought it was a bit strange as his clothing was still hanging in the closet and his personal items were on the dresser so I went back to the room. The vagrant was still knocking out the zeds as I looked through the drawers of the dresser for some idea to what had happened to my old mate. Both bottom drawers were empty but in the top one there was a snottery hanky and a couple of *syrup of figs* (wigs). I'd thought my old mucker must have been as bald as a badger's arse but he hid it well so why would he leave without his wigs? I picked one up for closer inspection only to have a wad of pound notes fall out from the hairy creature. There was about 30 quid held together with an elastic band and as he owed me six pounds I thought I should take it from the stash. Only the old bum was left in the room, and I was sure the money did not belong to him, so I left the wigs and took the cash. There was no reason for me to investigate the mystery of my missing mate any further so I did a runner. With the unexpected money from my bald bombardier and the cash I'd made on the curio box sale I was in good shape to get out of town. I packed all my belongings into a black bag and bought a ticket for St. Albans and was back in Belfast and the comfort of my own bed within 10 days.

CHAPTER 8

A Change in Direction

Returning home was great at first. It was coming up to Christmas and I was getting spoiled by my mum but by January things were bleak as I had no money and was unable to find work. I'd borrow 50 pence from my parents then go to the pub to play pool for pints and at 10 pence a game and 20 pence a pint I'd have to go home if I lost the first game. That was it for me: bored stiff without anywhere to go; London was bad but not this bad. What I loved about England was the freedom: no soldiers pulling you over, not being searched every time you entered a public building and no religious, sectarian nonsense. Jim had gotten his old job back on the lifts but when I asked him if they'd take me back there was no chance – something to do with the pile of electrical drawings I'd burnt when I had left. For me to get money it was down to selling stuff and scrounging off people after my dole money ran out or maybe nicking the odd bit of copper here and there. My old car was parked in the garage but there was no way I could sell that as I still owed my dad money to pay it off. I was fed up and going nowhere fast: getting into trouble, generally just becoming a waster, hanging around the pub.

One event really made me think about how messed up my life had become and made me realise that it needed to drastically change if I was to make anything of it. The night started off down the pub as any other Saturday would except on this occasion some of us had managed to get hold of a few gallon jugs of cheap cider that had come off a boat in the port of Larne. Usually when I got my dole money we'd have a couple of beers, then a crowd of us would go into town together for safety in numbers but this night was different. Wee Jim had called me to arrange a get-together at Johnny's house.

"*We've got some Larne cider,*" he said.

"*What does it taste like?*" I replied.

"*It's rattin', but it's cheap,*" he said laughing. That about summed it up: it was absolutely poison but the three of us polished off a few pints each in Johnny's bedroom before we went down to the pub to meet up with whoever else was hanging around. Most had headed off into town so not much would be happening in the bar. As we arrived outside the pub, Peter, an off duty reserve soldier, shouted to us across the car park:

"Who's going to Pig Pen?" This was a trendy nightspot in the countryside, about 10 miles to the north and occasionally we would go there but never without a decent crowd from the area. The more that went the safer it was. "The Pig" as it was locally known was very popular and attracted crowds from various parts of Belfast and they too would come mob-handed. I certainly did not want to go to the club with Peter as he was a real loose cannon. A lot of people carried guns but he was one of the few people that carried one legally and although he was great when sober he was a liability after a couple of pints and was prone to start waving his pistol around like John Wayne. This was a strong Loyalist area so no Catholics would be there, but that did not mean it would be a trouble-free night. There was always someone to fight with. As Jim, Johnny and I were about to enter the security gates outside the pub I heard a loud squawk.

"Are you lot goin' to the Pig?" yelled Big Roy as he got out of a black taxi.

"Aye maybe, what about you?"

"Aye me and Rab and probably my brother as well," he answered. There was not much sense in me driving up there as I was staggering a bit now that the cider had taken its toll. Drinking and driving was common then; most people didn't think about it, they would just drive, usually with an overloaded

vehicle. Besides my car would surely have been stolen by Roy's brother Dessie: he never used public transport, just nicked peoples cars; he'd taken mine three times already. He was a reasonable thief though; he always let me know where he had left it. Dessie was an uncontrollable *tea leaf but* not a bad sort, unlike his brother who could become quite unstable when upset. I thought if we went with this lot someone would certainly get *chinned* at some point of the evening at the Pig Pen.

Our local pub was completely surrounded by a large 12-foot steel fence. The only way in was through gates that led to a security hut where each person was searched before entering. My favourite watering hole had been blown up a few years earlier and had been rebuilt so safety measures were strict. We felt safer inside knowing everyone was searched first and that security was tight. One night, a bus load of drunken yahoos had tried to burst into the pub. The gates had been locked, keeping raiders out so we had had a good sideshow as we had watched the baboons attempt to climb the fence. Loud cheers had rung out as they had fallen off one by one after getting sliced up a treat by the barbed wire at the top. Normally the pub would empty and attack the invaders but there had not been enough of us that night so it had been wiser to lock them out.

You had to be wary about going into bars out of your area during the Troubles as someone would always spot an outsider amongst them. It was always best to be with someone from the vicinity as the locals were very particular about who entered their bar. Everybody knew each other so a strange face was a suspicious face. Eccentric people usually didn't last five minutes in the working class pubs of Belfast. Once a stranger came into the bar wearing a large cowboy type hat and waved to everyone; he got a good kicking then he and his hat were flung out into the street. He was guilty of two things: firstly he should not have waved, and he definitely should not have worn that hat. That was the way it was then.

Anyway, on this particular evening we had knocked back a couple of pints in the pub on top of the cider and the three of us were well on our way. Big Trevor stuck his head inside the alcove where we were sitting, and said:

"Who wants a lift to The Pig?" We jumped up and ran down to the car park behind him: it was first come first served. Trevor was one of the few people I knew who did not drink much so the chances of getting to where we were going in one piece were a lot higher when in his car. He only had a mini so with five squeezed inside it was not a very comfortable ride. There were four other carloads that also left

just after us so we would have a few from the estate present. The club was packed and the rules were: upstairs for dancing, downstairs for drinking. We stayed down. Another couple of pints and we were *blootered.*

"*Let's go upstairs now,*" said Jim; he was always keen to get sniffing for a bit of stuff.

"*Wait a wee minute,*" said Johnny as he downed a quick whiskey; he was having a big problem with his balance by then. We went upstairs, all of us well-oiled and ready to rock. A girl I knew from school waved to me as she danced about with a friend. I was so full of Dutch courage I was in like Flynn. My dancing was not much to behold and after a skin-full it was just plain nonsense but I was having a laugh and so were the girls. Then out of nowhere this clown jumped in between us and began bouncing around like an Orangutan with a banana up his arse. And I thought I couldn't dance!

"*Oi, what's your game?*" I yelled, moving back between them. He looked round at me and without warning planted a knuckle sandwich smack on my chin. I was knocked backwards, then regained my balance and jumped at him, landing the odd punch on his melon here and there. Before he could retaliate a couple of seven-foot gorillas doubling as bouncers grabbed the both of us and flung us down the fire escape into the car park. We both got up and he walked away. That was it as far as I was concerned: suddenly I was out of the club and all my mates were inside having a ball. There was not much to do except sit around and wait until the club shut down as it was miles from town with no way to get home. Drunk and discontented I slumped back against the wall then heard a voice.

"That's him." As I turned to hear who was talking – *bang!* – the sole of a large Doc Marten boot landed square on my face. Dazed, I tried to get up but – *whack!* – another kick landed on my head and sent me reeling. There were three of them and they all stuck the boot in. In my bloodied haze I remember seeing the snarling face of the yellow bastard that I had been scrapping with earlier: he had returned with some help and they were proceeding to kick me unconscious. An hour or so later someone found me lying in a pool of blood under the stairs of the fire escape and called an ambulance; the paramedics then connected me to a breathing apparatus. A mass brawl broke out at closing time when my mates found out what had happened. Apparently Roy started punching out anyone that was along with my attackers and Peter drew his gun and waved it wildly above his head: luckily the police arrived before he could use it. When I eventually regained consciousness the next day I was lying in a bed at the City Hospital.

A bright shaft of sunlight awakened me to a pounding headache as I struggled to open my eyes to see where I was. Only managing to squint I pulled myself from the bed with no recollection of what had previously happened but I was aware of the severe body pains that felt like I'd been trampled by a herd of buffalo. Bent over like Quasimodo, I hobbled to a bathroom to see what was left of my battered face. I had to turn around to see if someone was stood behind me as I did not recognize the cold stare of the distorted reflection in front of me. Both eyeballs were closed over, bruised and swollen, my nose was no longer in the centre of my face and my teeth protruded through my top lip. Apart from that I felt fine. With no memory of the past 24 hours I felt lost and afraid in that cold room but it was obvious that I had either been beaten up or in an accident. A nurse noticed my plight and helped me back to bed. Unknown to me my mum and dad were at the hospital but as I had been unconscious for over 10 hours they hadn't had the chance to speak to me. On their return later my mum almost fell apart when she saw what state I was in. Wee Jim had informed them what had happened the morning after and they had immediately gone up to the city hospital only to find me lying there, out for the count. They told me I had to stay in for another night for observation as I had a face like a busted onion, a broken nose, a couple of broken ribs and a concussion. The next morning I was still suffering, though not quite as bad, and I was able to move more freely without feeling like someone was jagging me with hot pokers. In the afternoon the doctor visited me to inform me I would be free to go after I had had my nose straightened. I asked him:

"How long will that take?" He leaned over close to me and replied:

"Not long," then in one swift movement grabbed my nose and wrenched it back into place, causing my eyeballs to erupt like the flow of Niagara Falls.

"There, you should be fine to leave within the hour," he said as he casually walked out of the ward.

A chilling account sent shivers all over me when my dad told me what had been disclosed when he had gone to the local police station close to the Pig Pen. He had been looking for some information about the attack and those responsible; the desk sergeant had offered condolences to my dad for his loss as he had been under the impression that I had died that night.

Back home I was in the capable hands of my mother during my convalescence. Over the past two years I had been involved in scuffles and I had sometimes ended up in hospital to receive a few stitches here and there but I had always been ready for the next encounter. This time was different: it had really frightened me and I became very anxious about leaving my house. For two or three weeks I stayed at home and with no job I was content to watch TV and let my mum spoil me. If I did go out it was just to sit on the wall of the front garden and watch the world go by.

My sister's fiancé Big Jim was keen to take revenge on the parties involved but I told him to let it go as I knew it would become a vicious circle of tit for tat. Those responsible stayed in their own area to lay low for a while as they expected a payback at any time though I'd convinced my mates that I didn't want to take it any further. Unknown to me Big Jim was already in pursuit of them and delivered retribution for me by sending a hit squad into their area to pick them up. It was severe: the main man who had picked me out in the car park that night ended up on crutches with his kneecaps busted; the others got a good kicking. There would be no comeback on this as they knew they had been dealt with by people high up the ladder and that retaliating would be suicide on their part. I hadn't wanted this but they had got what they'd deserved.

My friends would phone or call at the door to try and encourage me to leave the house but I was still nervous about the world outside my home. In due course I gradually went further down the road, to the sweet shop or the chippie for a fish supper. I remember my first trip into town after the beating was to see a football match and although intimidated by the crowd around me I enjoyed watching Linfield beat Waterford 3-0 with Alan McGraw getting a hat-trick in a friendly. Within about three months I was back down the pub or the Social Club but I had no intention of leaving the area as I was still a bag of nerves.

One night, I was playing pool when I was called over by Jeff – also known as The Beak – a guy I knew through mutual friends. He had lived in England for about six years and was now back home and I'd a have a drink with him from time to time. The Beak was about seven years older than me and could grow a moustache quicker than I could finish a pint of Guinness. I had gone to the same school as him starting the same year he had left and although older he was great *craic*. This simple get-together would be the reason I would eventually change my way of life for the better and it was all thanks to The Beak.

"The word's out that you took a heavy beating, I'm glad you're OK now," he said. I thanked him and pulled up a chair at his table. He continued:

"We're going to a party at Queen's University next week and I was wondering if you fancied a change of scenery, it would keep you out of trouble."

The last time I had been at the university had been to see *Lindisfarne* in 1972 with a few of my egghead school friends and that had been a great night so maybe it would be good to go along with them.

The following Friday I went to a disco in a hotel on the Coast Road near Carrickfergus. This was another first for me: my first time going to a nightclub since I had had my pan knocked in and once again I felt apprehensive. Wee Jim, Johnny, George and I met at the local pub before going to the disco. I thought I looked great in my new cream-coloured jacket, brown shirt and trousers with a pair of platform shoes. As we sat at a table near the bar a really drunken poncey type of person came staggering over to talk to us. He spoke directly to me.

"I know you, I'm The Beak's mate and we're going to Queen's tomorrow night." He was slurring and swaying and trying to align a Bloody Mary with his mouth. I'd never seen him in this pub before; he had been in the Social Club with The Beak the previous week but I had never conversed with him. None of my mates had met him before and they didn't seem too impressed by his antics: he was the type of drunk that could easily get chinned by anyone itching for a scrap. I tried to ignore him but he wouldn't go away then just as I was about to get up to go to the toilets he tried to put his arm

around me and spilt his Bloody Mary all over my lovely cream jacket.

"You stupid bastard, look what you've done!" I yelled. My mates jumped up, ready to take him on but I could see by his pathetic face that he had meant no harm and so I stopped any repercussions.

"Just go away before someone slaps you, and I'm not going to Queen's, especially with you," I moaned at him. I wiped my jacket in desperation but it was ruined: I could not go to the club dressed like a raspberry ripple. That was my first encounter with Michael, and one that could easily have been my last, but it was the first of many as he eventually became one of the best friends I ever had.

The Beak called the next day reminding me of the party at the university. We agreed to meet at the bar later to see how I felt about going. That evening I didn't arrange to see any of my usual mates and went down to the pub by myself hoping to go along with the flow of whatever occurred. There were only a handful of people in the lounge: The Beak and his friends were sitting cozily in the corner – one of them was Michael. That was all I needed; luckily I had worn old clothes but he stood up and apologized for his intoxicated performance the night before which was OK with me. The Beak introduced me to his other friends, all of whom I was meeting for the first time: Linda was with Michael and his next door neighbour Tom was with the other girl. Tom had lived in Reading, England at the same time as The Beak where they had played in a band together. They were all educated types, conversing about things such as the state of the world in general and the price of artichokes in the Spar: no mention of religion, football or fighting. This was a refreshing change and although I did more listening than talking the evening was enjoyable and before long a taxi arrived to take them into town. It didn't take much to coax me to go along with my new association so into the cab I jumped, heading for Queens University with people I hardly knew. As for The Beak, he'd left the pub after he'd pulled some old *slapper*. The party was a small affair held in one of the student residences with the entertainment coming from Michael and Tom performing a puppet show from behind a small cupboard. For most of the evening I was happy to stay in the background and let the others take the lead but it was pleasant and rewarding as I felt at ease with my newfound friends. These educated people would later take me to some strange educated parties and at one particular event I managed to make a fool of myself. It also made me think that I could be dyslexic: I went to a toga party dressed as a goat!

The next few months I began to split my time between my usual mates and The Beak's lot, and as a result I managed to stay out of trouble. Trips to places that I had not been to since I was a kid were common with my new friends as Linda and Michael both had cars. One evening we went to Newcastle, County Down with Michael dressed as an Arab, complete with false tan. We bought a carry-out then nicked a boat and cruised out into the harbour as sightseers watched in disbelief at the sight of an Arab at the helm. Michael was always playing practical jokes and the more I was with him the more I liked him. Sometimes though he went a bit too far as on this occasion – or he would have done if we had not stopped him from attempting to sail the boat to England. He was educated to 'A' level standard and worked as an accountant and therefore was the first person I'd met who had a cheque book so I thought he was rich. Behind all his joviality he was a sad person: his dad had committed suicide three years earlier and the last time they'd spoken had been during an argument. Michael had found his dad dead the next day in the garage with a pipe connected to the exhaust run inside the car. He had never fully recovered from that shock.

Linda rented a caravan in Portrush for two weeks to get away from it all along with her friends, the two Irenes. One of them was a girl I'd known from school and the other was an ex-girlfriend of mine who had blown me out a couple of years before. This was supposed to be a ladies getaway but Michael rented a van and invited me, along with The Beak, Tom and an old friend, Bill, to gate crash their peaceful retreat for a weekend. By the time of our arrival in Portrush we were all in a merry state after enjoying a few mouthfuls each of the carry-out from the off-license we had purchased for the weekend. And we no longer had to put up with Bill's dreadful voice, as he eventually passed out. During the trip, every time he had taken a drink from his large whisky bottle he insisted on standing up to belt out *Pearl's a Singer*. He wasn't quite in the same league as Elkie Brooks.

The resort was nestled in a beautiful spot at Whitepark Bay and it overlooked the Irish Sea to the Mull of Kintyre in Scotland: a place that I had not visited since my childhood days. It felt like all the bad times had been left behind for a while, with the worries of gangs, religious strife and the Troubles put on hold. We'd go down to the beach to take in the sea air and laze around or kick a ball about – well not Michael: he had two left feet and kept falling over. The girls went canoeing, along with Tom and me: another thing I had not done since my scouting days. I was really content then and even had a second fling with Irene. The decision to be more selective with my choice of friends had resulted in a completely new lifestyle and attitude. Four months earlier I'd been contemplating getting back out of Northern Ireland but all seemed just about right at that moment.

If we did cause some bother it was not premeditated, such as a day in the lounge at Kelly's Club in Portrush. It started to rain heavily and the bar began to fill up with people seeking shelter. The Beak pulled out his guitar that he always had with him and jumped up onto the pool table for better effect. Bill also climbed onto the table accompanied by two pretty girls who began to go-go dance. The place was rocking with everyone singing along until Bill brought the house down – or should I say the ceiling – when he leaped from the table to grab one of the chandeliers for a Tarzan-like swing. The forward motion was perfect but on the back swing he came crashing to the floor as he tore out the expensive light fixture along with a chunk of the ceiling. He received a huge roar of approval but predictably the bar was soon cleared by the enraged staff. Foolish but enjoyable entertainment.

With very little involvement in the everyday Belfast strife I found myself looking forward to each weekend and my next new thrilling escapade with my zany and fashionable bunch of friends. Davy C. had returned from New Zealand – minus my shoes – so we had a bit of catching up to do particularly concerning his covert exit from London. Then one

Saturday a tragedy occurred that tore apart not only the people directly involved but also most of the estate. This was another extremely traumatic experience for me and it left a deep emotional scar within me for a long period; even now I sometimes have flashbacks so vivid I feel like I could touch them.

On the night that this tragedy occurred I spent the time drinking in the local pub, mingling with a collection of different friends and not sitting with any group in particular. By the end of the night I was with Wee Jim, Michael, Davy C., and a friend called Wally, when someone suggested that we should go for a Chinese take-away. It was a short walk to the restaurant: a popular spot at the end of the night for stragglers from the pub and the Social Club. We were all in good spirits, laughing and joking as we strolled back and tucked into our Oriental fare. Suddenly an altercation behind us between two people who were continuously feuding caught our attention. Someone shouted:

"They're fighting again; we'd better stop it before they do each other in!"

We began running back towards the fray to pull them apart. All of us were on the footpath but Wally was just on the roadside close to the edge. A car behind screeched then skidded and as I looked around Wally was hit on his right-hand side and launched into the air with his head hitting the curb when he landed. The car slowed down, stopped, and then sped off. He lay motionless, struggling for breath; there was no blood and he was extremely pale. Michael took off his long brown leather jacket and placed it under Wally's head to give him some comfort. I was rubbing his face and talking to him trying to get a response. It seemed like hours but the ambulance finally arrived to take him to the hospital. We could not get Wally to come round and as he was lifted onto the stretcher his eyes flickered and he gave out a long guttural groan. Then his eyes closed again. Despondent we dispersed and went our own ways, not knowing the severity of Wally's injury. The next morning my mind blanked as I tried to piece together the previous night. My dad shook me to say my friend Steven was on the phone which was strange as he rarely called. I raised the phone to my ear.

"You were with Wally last night?"

"Aye," I replied. *"How is he?"*

"He's dead," was his answer. I dropped the phone, and then wandered to my room in disbelief. I reflected on the gasping groan he had made just as they had lifted him onto the stretcher and realized that we had watched him die. A good friend had been lost right in front of my eyes and I was numb. The days between his death and the funeral

were solemn; we lived on a big housing estate but in reality it was a small close-knit community. All the animosity and aggression people normally had for each other was put on hold as we mourned. The funeral was much like any other funeral although for the family losing a son at 18 was devastating. Time was a great healer and eventually we all got back into our routines. I began to distance myself from my old mates to spend more time with The Beak, Bill and Michael, and although things were good again the image of Wally's death was constant.

After being out of work for about three months my dad got me a job with a company that fitted out and repaired police cars on the Lisburn Road. Apart from friends who could keep a secret the line of work that I was to be doing would be unknown to anyone else. As far as the rest of the world was concerned I was working for RE Hamilton's, a Ford dealership on the opposite side of the road. Helping out the police with their duties could make anyone a potential target for the IRA so my work had to be kept hush-hush if I wanted to continue as part of the human race. My role was extremely important in keeping her majesty's Royal Ulster Constabulary ticking along smoothly; I had the distinguished position of assistant to the assistant to the parts manager. There were not many who could grab a 1976 Ford Granada clutch from a shelf and pass it on to someone who would then pass it on to someone else. But it was a job and a wage packet so I had a chance to save for a new car to replace my Wolseley Hornet that had been sold off to repay my dad. Once again he helped me purchase my next vehicle with a trip to Bangor to pick up a two-door 1969 white and black Vauxhall Viva HB. At last: back on the road again.

On the weekends I'd pick my mates up and head to the coast, sometimes driving onto the Larne-Stranraer ferry for a pint in Scotland; it was good to be behind the wheel again. Owning a car had an expensive disadvantage: having to pay for repairs. The old Vauxhall was running fine but as with all cars the task of stopping was quite important. The Viva did not have this function. Michael had a cousin living a few miles away in Ballyclare who dabbled in auto repairs and who had offered to fix up the brakes for a reasonable price the next Saturday morning. I picked up Michael from Linda's new flat which was right beside Bill's flat: perfect for future parties. Bill wanted to come along for the drive and The Beak had called Bill to see what he was doing and to ask if he could also go. As we drove to pick them up two other acquaintances were walking along: Reid and a fellow called Spence, who always dressed in a long white raincoat. We pulled over. They got in and by the time we left for Ballyclare there were seven of us in the car including Fat Marky who had somehow wormed his way into the action. After a really slow drive we arrived and unloaded the others at the Square Bar where Marky's uncle worked; then Michael took me to see his cousin. Unfortunately we had turned up late to find he wasn't there so we went back to the bar. I had one pint whilst the others had about five before they ordered some cider for the journey back. Driving home watching my passengers swigging back cider and getting *blootered* gave me an uneasy feeling that the trip may not end well. Sure enough moments later I looked in my rear-view mirror to see a police Landrover behind and as we approached our turn-off things became a bit erratic. Just before the intersection I indicated to turn right and eased over to the centre lane, preparing for the unknown, but the car wouldn't slow down. Taking evasive action I cancelled the right turn signal and kept going straight ahead and attempted to regain the inside lane. Checking my mirror I could see the police driver flicking on his emergency lights as he sped up alongside and pointed for me to pull over. The Landrover overtook and stopped up ahead. Again another attempt to halt the car proved futile and I swerved around the Landrover to avoid a collision and glanced over helplessly to see them engaging the bolts of their Sterling submachine guns. At that time the policy was to shoot at any vehicle that ran through a checkpoint and although this had not exactly been the case it was definitely debatable. Once more they pulled up alongside, guns at the ready, demanding we should stop before maneuvering to the front of the Vauxhall and causing me to swerve towards the roadside. Before they had any thoughts of opening fire I dragged the car to the left and ran it up a grassy bank at the side of the road to stop. Instantly the police team jumped from the Landrover, pointing their guns directly at the car and yelling for us to put our arms in the air. One cop opened the passenger side door, which created a spillage of drunks and empty cider bottles onto the ground at the feet of the officers. They stepped back in astonishment as one by one we clambered out of the car. Spence had used to be in the police reserve and insisted that we let him do the talking.

"*OK, I know our rights, I was in the forces, stop pointing your guns at us as I've got your badge numbers.*"

One cop replied:

"*Shut up Colombo or we'll plug you first.*" So he shut up. The Beak was still in the backseat drinking cider when another cop spotted him.

"*Oi, who's that still in there, get him out, he looks like a Mexican bandit.*"

He was dragged out to stand in line with the rest of us as the police did a head count and began asking our names and occupations. None of us had spoken since Spence had opened his big trap; all the while I was thinking they were going to throw the book at me. Fat Marky didn't help when he was asked for his personal information. With confidence he said:

"I'm Richard Reginald Markson the third and I'm a horticultural engineer." In reality he was Fat Marky and cut grass for the council. The sergeant ignored him, then approached me when he found out that the car was mine and said:

"Driving with no brakes, overloading the car and failing to stop when requested, that could be a hefty fine, I'll be back when I check you all out."

License in hand he called me over and looked at my name and address to ask if Harry was any relation and I reluctantly informed him that he was my dad. He then advised me to rejoin my partners in crime who were still lined up on the roadside. Another Landrover arrived at the scene, loaded four of us into the back and drove away, leaving Reid, Michael and myself to climb into the other vehicle to be taken to somewhere unknown. At the bottom of the estate they dropped Reid and Michael off and took me further up the road, where they stopped at a petrol station. The sergeant pushed his face within inches of mine and said:

"Get a tow truck to pick up your car tomorrow and don't drive it until it's fixed, no charges. Now get out, it's lucky we know your da!"

Once again my dad had inadvertently come to the rescue but he never mentioned if he had been made aware of this episode. The car was towed home the next day and left parked up for a while until sufficient funds were made available to fix it.

Over the next couple of months my weekends were mainly spent at Bill or Linda's flat, as I slept in one or the other. One night, well-lubricated after a session at the pub I made my one step forward, two steps backwards stroll to Bill's place. Alas there was no answer to my quiet, noisy tapping on the door so I used my master breaking and entering skills to get through a window and collapsed onto the living room floor. Whilst tossing and turning on the floor trying to get comfortable I began to notice that his fish tank was missing and that all of the furniture and photographs were different. Something was not right: everything had changed since the last weekend, and Bill's place must have had a complete makeover. The answer to this enigma became apparent by the lack of empty beer bottles, the clean kitchen and the vase of flowers on the table. I was in the wrong flat! Panic set in as I silently tiptoed to the front door and out onto the landing; then I was off like Speedy Gonzales down the road. It had been a lucky escape as the neighbour on the other side was a knife-wielding maniac and could have sliced me up a treat.

Times were virtually uncomplicated for me since changing my outlook on how to live my life in Northern Ireland, mainly due to the company that I now kept. Although I'd managed to stay out of bother and hadn't been slapped about for a few months everything could suddenly change in a Belfast minute during the Troubles. Terrorist activities were in full-swing and lives were still being routinely destroyed or lost, just as mine nearly was after an explosion on my way to work. One day I was driving along, thinking about the great goal I'd scored at the weekend when ahead of me a building blew-up without warning. The explosion caused a bus to lose control and the driver crashed into a shop front, leaving windows shattered and passengers bloodied, screaming in distress.

The chain reaction produced by the blast resulted in out-of-control drivers colliding with each other and my car bouncing up onto the footpath and narrowly avoiding a telephone box. Fortunately the only damage for me was soiled underpants, a busted headlight and a flat tyre. This incident made me aware that even staying away from the turmoil was not a guarantee of a safe passage during those times

My old mates were still around and we'd have a laugh now and again but some of them were becoming very disruptive and were still involved in a lot of irregularity. I had gradually begun to leave all that aggravation behind: I was content with eating, drinking and being merry instead of drinking, throwing up and fighting. Travelling around the countryside living life in the slow lane had become more appealing than hanging around the city. Michael's girlfriend Linda was usually with us which was great as she became the constant designated driver who took us from pub to pub and other scenic venues. Sometimes she'd bring my old girlfriend Irene along and although there was a slight possibility of us making another go of it I was wary of getting blown out for a second time so we played it casual. We'd cross paths occasionally on a trips to Linda's caravan at the coastal town of Newcastle where Michael would often invite us to visit without the permission of the owner.

The Beak had a strange hippie type friend, Ted, visit from England and it was quite entertaining watching him stand out like a sore thumb as he bumbled around the pub or Social Club. One night The Beak, Ted, Michael and I climbed into Linda's car in the pub car park ready to go to a club in Carrickfergus. Just as Linda started the engine a drunken *eejit* that had earlier tried to hitch a lift with us came out of the pub demanding to let him into the car. Linda told Ted to wind his passenger window down so she could tell him again to get lost and as we started to move Ted received a kung fu kick right on the kisser, which caused his face to shoot blood and snotters into the air. The Beak and I bailed out to confront the drunken assailant who went down easily from an uppercut by The Beak and ended up absorbing a few more slaps from us as he tried to counter. Staff from the pub saw the commotion occurring and dragged the wounded aggressor away for his own safety. As Linda attended to Ted's plight a tall man wearing a black leather jacket crossed the road and stood a couple of yards from us. He reached into his inside pocket and drew a handgun which he raised to point at The Beak and me. Then he asked,

"What's the problem here, is there something that needs sorted?"

"It's all taken care of," I said.

"Talk to big Alec in the pub, he'll give you the details." With that he swung the gun back into his jacket, spun around and marched on down the road like a soldier on guard outside Buckingham Palace. Linda, Michael and I were joined by Bill and

we proceeded on to the club; The Beak took Ted back to his mum's house for a bit of dental and mouth repair. Welcome to Belfast, mister funny wee English man.

Ted's love affair with Ulster would not be completed until he was arrested, and that didn't take long. The next weekend Michael and I took Ted into the city for a night out. He looked confused and nervous as we approached the large spiked metal security railings that ringed the main streets of the town centre dotted with turn styles. It was like entering a zoo but here the main sights were a few crazy drunks acting like animals. The railings didn't prevent rivals from going for each other's throats when on the inside, though the attacks were significantly reduced. Also the area was safer due to the fact that each person was searched upon entering and cars were not allowed in as they were a favourite source of bomb transportation. Michael had overdosed on Crème de Menthe and had begun to act bizarrely, prancing around the large concrete flower potholders, determined to make the city pretty, like a constipated Morris dancer. He pulled out one of the plants and bashed me over the head then slung a load of soil at Ted. I retaliated by chasing him up the street and flinging another dislodged plant in his direction only to see it make a direct hit on a policeman's chest as he turned the corner. Within seconds the cops had us on the ground surrounded by what seemed like the first battalion of the Argyle and Sutherland Highlanders. We were slung into an awaiting Landrover and carted off to the nearby Musgrave Street police station. After an hour of pleading with the desk sergeant in order to convince him that our English friend was over on holiday and completely innocent Ted was released onto the streets. They sent him into the night; he was confused and had no idea of his whereabouts or how to get back to our estate. He ended up walking in the wrong direction through the Republican Markets area and found a cab to take him to The Beak's house. He was lucky to get out of town alive and lucky that the cab driver – undoubtedly driving a black taxi for the IRA – would take him back to a strong Protestant area. After giving statements and generally being kept for no reason in separate locked rooms for two hours they let us go and arranged a future courthouse appointment. On the day of our appearance in court I was still hopeful of getting off as I'd sort of assured my mum and dad that no further trouble would be expected. We stood in the dock awaiting the prosecutors' speech with my statement being the first to be dealt with.

"Your honour on the first page of accused number one's statement he goes on at length of

how he was defending himself from a rival gang that had attacked him with some horticultural weapons. On pages three, four and five he describes how they were being chased when the officer was hit by the plant from the rival gang. No other gang members were ever found despite the large army presence at the scene. The last two pages seem to repeat the first five; it just goes on and on." He placed my essay on the desk then prepared himself to read out Michael's statement to the court.

"A childish prank under the euphor, euphor?" He paused and leaned over to a clerk and showed him the document; the clerk whispered into his ear then the prosecutor continued.

"A childish prank under the euphoria of alcohol." The judge looked up then banged his gavel.

"Both fined 20 pounds, NEXT!" That was that: unable to convince the crown that we were victims. The court gave us a month to pay and as I was only earning 10 pounds a week it would have been a struggle for me to come up with the money without my parents' help. Michael told me not to worry as he whipped out his cheque book and filled in 40 quid on the dotted line, saying that there was no rush to pay the money back. I looked at him and thought he must have been a millionaire.

One day Big Jim called me and asked if we could meet up as there was something urgent he wanted to discuss. I thought it a bit strange as although we were good friends our social activities very rarely crossed over as his tended to involve intimidation, aggravated assault, skullduggery or just plain badness. Sometimes though he was just having a laugh with one example of his less serious illicit behaviour being the caper of the mysterious missing goalposts. He was a good footballer and had just started a new team in the area where they had flattened a bit of land and had made a decent pitch; now they needed posts. One night he and a few of his mates decided to borrow – without the owner's consent – a flatbed lorry to take to the local playing fields. The idea at the field was again to borrow – this time permanently – a set of goalposts from one of the pitches to install in their freshly constructed one. They went at night like all good thieves would do and as they attempted to remove the posts a large sweeping spotlight lit up the entire field: he had been caught by the army. After a brief discussion informing the squaddies that the posts were being moved under instructions of the council the soldiers helped them uproot them and even went along to finish the installation at the new pitch. Maybe they thought it would be cheaper if the council worked at night in the dark – who knows?

Something big was on Jim's mind so we went for a stroll through the estate where he told me of his intentions to marry my sister and asked how I felt about it. He knew there would be a problem considering my dad's involvement with the police and his with the underworld. His status in the paramilitaries was emerging as he grew bigger and stronger and he was destined to go even higher and this would certainly lead to problems later on. Kathleen had never let me believe that she was close to marrying Jim but I knew if they kept seeing each other it would be a distinct possibility. While slightly unprepared for Big Jim to be my future brother-in-law I definitely did not anticipate that he would ask me to be best man. After this revelation we went to the pub and got drunk. Finally Jim proposed and although there was initial concern from my parents they knew the marriage was inevitable so the wedding plans went into action. Soon my sister and Jim had a house arranged to move into before they had even got married so things were moving along smoothly – but the stag night was still to come.

On that particular evening we met at the pub close to where their new house was. Some of my good mates had gone to school with Jim but hadn't had much contact with him since they'd started working so none of them were there. I knew a few of the lads from around the area but a lot of the people there were scary big bastards from the UDA that had recently been released from jail or would be going there soon. One of them was Big Jake, a hairy Neanderthal with mad eyes and a ginger beard who had just completed a manslaughter sentence for slicing someone up a treat in Glasgow. Nice fellow though. After about six pints we were off mob-handed to a local cigarette factory social club that had been rented for the evening. Most of the night was taken up by singing and heavy drinking with not much bother apart from a few broken glasses. Then all hell broke loose close to the midnight hour. The front doors were busted in by a crowd wielding wooden batons and iron bars that made a beeline towards us. Just like general Custer Big Jim circled the wagons in defense, grabbing bottles and glasses before tipping over the tables to use them as shields. It was pandemonium as we clashed with the unknown foe: blood and snotters everywhere. Amongst all the chaos Jim still had time to make sure I was behind the front ranks as he knew it was getting real bad. Two or three of the criminally insane from our group jumped the defending wall of tables to confront the aggressors full on, taking blow after blow to the head. I found shelter behind the bar with a few others and we were able to use a supply of beer bottles to lob them like hand grenades into the fray. Just when it seemed certain we would all soon get our heads panned in another group of about 20 people piled in through the doors and proceeded to beat the living shit out of our attackers. Who were this lot? Over at the side entrance a hooded figure was gesturing to us and pointing at an awaiting van. We left the others to continue the battle and loaded ourselves into the van to be whisked away from the club, making sure to avoid a second parked van that had transported our relief squadron. As we turned onto the main road four or five police cars screeched past on their way to the club. We ended the night in Big Jake's second floor flat where we were provided with a feast of beans and toast, after all our wounds had been attended to. I sat in the corner totally bewildered by what had just occurred, listening to the group already planning revenge on the assailants from Carrick. This gang had been waiting for some time to get their chance to take out Big Jim, but had again failed. To round an insane evening off Jake collected everyone's dishes and promptly flung them out the window onto the street below. Just an average night out with Big Jim.

The wedding was the next day and luckily we had received no facial wounds so we were able to continue on with no one from my family any the wiser of the recent events. Still feeling a bit drunk

I was awakened by Jim calling me from downstairs. It was late and we didn't have much time to get to the church. We both put on our suits and waited for one of Jim's mates to pick us up. Pacing about nervously he grabbed a bottle of QC wine from the cupboard and held it up, then smiled at me on his way out to the back garden. I followed him out and we both sat down on the wall to polish it off before the pick-up. By the time we got to the church we were almost drunk again, both of us sitting in the front pew with our heads in our hands waiting for everyone else to arrive. It was best man again for me: back at the same church as the previous year when I had stood beside Billy. This time though the alcohol was greatly affecting my stance as I swayed at the altar. There was a possibility of me falling over with the ring in my hand as Kathleen began her beautiful march up the aisle holding my proud father's arm. The ceremony was great as was the reception at a close by hotel with friends and family congregating for the happy occasion. My mother seemed impressed by a very nice, polite Scottish fellow with a beard: I think his name was Big Jake. Everything after my speech was a write-off due to over indulgence at the bar as I had sat listening to radio coverage of Northern Ireland losing 2-1 to England at Windsor Park. They were unlucky not to get their first victory for over 50 years since a certain football immortal; Tucker Croft had scored a famous winner in 1923. Chris McGrath saw his early strike cancelled by a Mick Channon equalizer and although a draw would have been a fair result Denis Tueart netted the winner for England with five minutes remaining. The best man's speech was a disaster, though it was rescued by one of my cousins John H., who helped me during my drunken slur and eased my embarrassment. One of my old girlfriends helped with my demeanor through the remainder of the evening and later managed to get me home safely. That was the third time in as many years that I had had the honour of being best man and each time I had failed as I had been too terrified to carry out my duties in a sober, responsible manner. No one ever asked me again which was probably just as well as each of the three couples split up within two years.

My tedious and boring job was driving me nuts and I wanted to quit: it was becoming soul-destroying. The only bit of relief came each Thursday when a couple of us had to go down the Lisburn Road to the bank to collect the wages. We would usually take a Ford Granada police car ready for patrol and speed down the road humming the theme tune of *The Sweeney* but that was as good as it got. All this monotony was put on hold one day with a gruesome delivery. When a police car came in for repairs my job would sometimes entail me to go over and pick up the paperwork from the vehicle for the parts that were required. On this day a few of us were called to help unload a high profile car from a flatbed truck that had been involved in police fatalities. The Ford Cortina was covered with a tarpaulin that was to be removed only when the car had been unloaded and locked in a secured enclosure. Our job was to make sure it was not tampered with as it was to be examined by a forensic team from England. We wondered what all the high security was for but were shocked by what was revealed when the covering was removed. The car was silver but it was difficult to distinguish the colour as there was very little metal on the car that hadn't been pierced by machine gun shells. It was just like a giant colander. Four policemen had died during an ambush in the countryside in which the IRA had used multiple automatic weapons. The interior was splattered with flesh and brain matter from the unsuspecting officers who hadn't stood a chance and we stood in silence, frozen. Years of growing up in our crazy world of conflict and mayhem had hardened a lot of people; bombs and gunfire had become normal. You just kept on going. I'd seen some horrific things over the last few years so nothing much really bothered me anymore but standing by that car left me cold.

Even though things for me were generally okay – staying out of trouble and enjoying my after-work activities – I became restless and felt like it was time to get away from Belfast again. Flashbacks of that bullet-ridden car kept me awake at night wondering how any human could be so merciless. Did they actually delight in taking the lives of these helpless human beings? They had been someone's sons or fathers and most chillingly: it could have been my father. Ulster was home to some evil people and I had to get away from it.

The Beak was planning a trip back to Reading for the pop festival and he was thinking about staying for a month or two and maybe picking up some casual work. Michael, Bill and one of his friends Ian had all showed interest in going and they asked if I wanted to join them. The timing was right for me and although I'd no idea where Reading was situated I did know they were struggling in 16th place in the old 3rd division. Nevertheless they had given Arsenal a run for their money in the FA Cup a couple of years previously, with Pat Rice scoring a lucky winner of a long range deflected shot. The plan was for The Beak and Ian to go over and stay with friends one month before the festival and then for Michael and Bill to come over just before it started. I agreed to go with them on the advance party and looked forward to handing my notice in at work. The week before my last day on the job my old Vauxhall's engine blew up about a mile from the workshop. Getting the thing towed away would be pricey, let alone fixing it, so I took out the radio and battery and left it on the roadside. Within a week of abandoning the car it had been gradually picked clean: first the wheels then the doors and before long all that was left was the chassis and that went too within the next couple of days. My last day of work was on Thursday, July 7th 1977, (7/7/77) and unknown to me then it would be my last pay slip ever in Northern Ireland.

The trip to Reading was only supposed to be for a few months, so I always expected to return and settle down after finding work in the Belfast area. Two days later I packed a bag and waited for Linda and Michael to pick me and the others up to take us to the airport. My mum was in a terrible state, crying her eyes out, but at that age although also sad I was selfishly thinking of myself and the events ahead. Because the venture was supposed to be for a short time I really didn't say goodbye to anyone in particular. The idea of leaving my mum permanently seemed ridiculous so I tried to comfort her with the thought that I'd be back within a couple of months.

The excitement of future adventures gave me a high as the adrenaline rushed through my body when I boarded the plane. We were all in great spirits as the Boeing 737 roared along the runway before lifting off and rising into the scattered clouds hanging over Lough Neagh. I had an inside seat and a great view of the Belfast rooftops glistening in the sporadic shafts of sunlight that danced on the city below. My heart fluttered momentarily as we sat silently during the plane's ascent. What was there ahead of me? Although my intention was to stay away for only a few months there was a distinct possibility that the situation could change to a longer drawn-out affair.

Just then I felt like a little boy again: frightened and unsure of my actions as I envisioned my mum at home crying for her son. Was I making a serious mistake? My parents were upset but they knew it was better to lose me temporarily than to have me grow up in such an unpredictable climate. It was safer in England. The pilot banked the plane to the left as if to give me a final glimpse of my home as we straightened up and flew right above the estate and made our way out onto the Irish Sea. The streets looked hospitable and calm from my lofty perception and it seemed as if I was from another world observing this marvellous sight from a serene angle. Glancing to the top of the estate my mind drifted back to the innocent times of my early days: days filled with so much joy as I had toddled along and progressed merrily into adolescence. Going up the Hill, playing in the Muckies or the endless fun at Mackies: it was all there to be absorbed fleetingly from above as the years were broken down into a matter of seconds.

Looking southward I took a deep breath and held onto the arms of my seat as the city began to disappear from view. As everything flashed by I thought of all of the people who I had grown up with: they were still there on the streets below but I was leaving them all behind as the need for change had grown inside me. We had stood together through the traumatic times, as we had lost people close to us as the beautiful city of our past had been methodically destroyed. Gunfire and explosions were now a way of life that everyone in Northern Ireland sadly took for granted and I was bidding it a painful goodbye as I flew off into the unknown. Piece by piece the scene changed as everything rushed by me at 100 miles per hour: first the rows of terraced houses; then the fields and football pitches and the bars and the clubs; until finally all I could see was the array of busy sea vessels leaving or entering Belfast Lough. Then that was gone too.

The Beak nudged me from my trance to ask if everything was okay. I nodded feebly as I attempted to reassure him. He asked me:

"What are you thinking?"

I looked out the window towards the horizon and then back to his ugly mug. There were so many thoughts in my head and I was unable to answer the question. So I turned back to the window and replied:

"Nothing. Just wondering about tomorrow."

The end

CPSIA information can be obtained
at www.ICGtesting.com
Printed in the USA
BVOW11s1105210316
441132BV00032B/615/P